S0-BON-788

SSF

	DATE DUE		

The Growth and Influence of Islam

In the Nations of Asia and Central Asia

Bangladesh

The Growth and Influence of Islam
IN THE NATIONS OF ASIA AND CENTRAL ASIA

Afghanistan

Azerbaijan

Bangladesh

Indonesia

Islam in Asia: Facts and Figures

Islamism and Terrorist Groups in Asia

Kazakhstan

The Kurds

Kyrgyzstan

Malaysia

Muslims in China

Muslims in India

Muslims in Russia

Pakistan

Tajikistan

Turkmenistan

Uzbekistan

The Growth and Influence of Islam
IN THE NATIONS OF ASIA AND CENTRAL ASIA

Bangladesh

Doris Valliant

Mason Crest Publishers
Philadelphia

Produced by OTTN Publishing, Stockton, New Jersey

Mason Crest Publishers
370 Reed Road
Broomall, PA 19008
www.masoncrest.com

First printing

1 3 5 7 9 8 6 4 2

Library of Congress Cataloging-in-Publication Data

Valliant, Doris.
  Bangladesh / Doris Valliant.
      p. cm. — (Growth and influence of Islam in the nations of Asia and
Central Asia)
  Includes bibliographical references and index.
  ISBN 1-59084-879-9
  1. Bangladesh—Juvenile literature. I. Title. II. Series.
  DS393.4.V25 2005
  954.92--dc22

                                        2005002754

Table of Contents

Dr. Harvey Sicherman, president and director of the Foreign Policy Research Institute, is the author of such books as America the Vulnerable: Our Military Problems and How to Fix Them (2002) and Palestinian Autonomy, Self-Government and Peace (1993).

Introduction

by Dr. Harvey Sicherman

America's triumph in the Cold War promised a new burst of peace and prosperity. Indeed, the decade between the demise of the Soviet Union and the destruction of September 11, 2001, proved deceptively hopeful. Today, of course, we are more fully aware—to our sorrow—of the dangers and troubles no longer just below the surface.

The Muslim identities of most of the terrorists at war with the United States have also provoked great interest in Islam as well as the role of religion in politics. It is crucial for Americans not to assume that Osama bin Laden's ideas are identical to those of most Muslims or, for that matter, that most Muslims are Arabs. A truly world religion, Islam claims hundreds of millions of adherents, from every ethnic group scattered across the globe. This book series covers the growth and influence of Muslims in Asia and Central Asia.

A glance at the map establishes the extraordinary coverage of our authors. Every climate and terrain may be found, along with every form of human society, from the nomadic groups of the Central Asian steppes to highly sophisticated cities such as Singapore, New Delhi, and Shanghai. The

A young Bangladeshi Muslim joins her elders in morning prayers outside the Baitul Mukarram National Mosque in Dhaka. More than 8 in 10 Bangladeshis—over 100 million people in all—are adherents of Islam.

economies of the nations examined in this series are likewise highly diverse. In some, barter systems are still used; others incorporate modern stock markets. In some of the countries, large oil reserves hold out the prospect of prosperity. Other countries, such as India and China, have progressed by moving from a government-controlled to a more market-based economic system. Still other countries have built wealth on service and shipping.

Central Asia and Asia is a heavily armed and turbulent area. Three of its states (China, India, and Pakistan) are nuclear powers, and one (Kazakhstan) only recently rid itself of nuclear weapons. But it is also a place where the horse and mule remain indispensable instruments of war. All of the region's states have an extensive history of conflict, domestic and international, old and new. Afghanistan, for example, has known little but invasion and civil war over the past two decades.

Governments include dictatorships, democracies, and hybrids without a name; centralized and decentralized administrations; and older patterns of tribal and clan associations. The region is a veritable encyclopedia of political expression.

Although such variety defies easy generalities, it is still possible to make several observations. First, the geopolitics of Central Asia and Asia reflect the impact of empires and the struggles of post-imperial independence. Central Asia, a historic corridor for traders and soldiers, was the scene of Russian expansion well into Soviet times. While Kazakhstan's leaders participated in the historic meeting of December 25, 1991, that dissolved the Soviet Union, the rest of the region's newly independent republics hardly expected it. They have found it difficult to grapple with a sometimes tenuous independence, buffeted by a strong residual Russian influence, the absence of settled institutions, the temptation of newly valuable natural resources, and mixed populations lacking a solid national identity. The shards of the Soviet Union have often been sharp—witness the Russian war in Chechnya—and sometimes fatal for those ambitious to grasp them.

Moving further east, one encounters an older devolution, that of the half-century since the British Raj dissolved into India and Pakistan (the latter giving violent birth to Bangladesh in 1971). Only recently, partly under the impact of the war on terrorism, have these nuclear-armed neighbors and adversaries found it possible to renew attempts at reconciliation. Still further east, Malaysia shares a British experience, but Indonesia has been influenced by its Dutch heritage. Even China defines its own borders along the lines of the Qing empire (the last pre-republican dynasty) at its most expansionist (including Tibet and Taiwan). These imperial histories lie heavily upon the politics of the region.

A second aspect worth noting is the variety of economic experimentation afoot in the area. State-dominated economic strategies, still in the ascendant, are separating government from the actual running of commerce and industry. "Privatization," however, is frequently a byword for crony capitalism and corruption. Yet in dynamic economies such as that of China, as well as an increasingly productive India, hundreds of millions of people have dramatically improved both their standard of living and their hope for the future. All of them aspire to benefit from international trade. Competitive advantages, such as low-cost labor (in some cases trained in high technology) and valuable natural resources (oil, gas, and minerals), promise much. This is indeed a revolution of rising expectations, some of which are being satisfied.

Yet more than corruption threatens this progress. Population increase, even though moderating, still overwhelms educational and employment opportunities. Many countries are marked by extremes of wealth and poverty, especially between rural and urban areas. Dangerous jealousies threaten ethnic groups (such as anti-Chinese violence in Indonesia). Hopelessly overburdened public services portend turmoil. Public health, never adequate, is harmed further by environmental damage to critical resources (such as the Aral Sea). By and large, Central Asian and Asian countries are living well beyond their infrastructures.

Third and finally, Islam has deeply affected the states and peoples of the region. Indonesia is the largest Muslim state in the world, and India hosts the second-largest Muslim population. Islam is not only the official religion of many states, it is the very reason for Pakistan's existence. But Islamic practices and groups vary: the well-known Sunni and Shiite groups are joined by energetic Salafi (Wahabi) and Sufi movements. Over the last 20 years especially, South and Central Asia have become battlegrounds for competing Shiite (Iranian) and Wahabi (Saudi) doctrines, well financed from abroad and aggressively antagonistic toward non-Muslims and each other. Resistance to the Soviet invasion of Afghanistan brought these groups battle-tested warriors and organizers. The war on terrorism has exposed just how far-reaching and active the new advocates of holy

Poverty is rampant in Bangladesh. Here a woman begs on the streets of Dhaka.

war (jihad) can be. Indonesia, in particular, is the scene of rivalry between an older, tolerant Islam and the jihadists. But Pakistan also faces an Islamic identity crisis. And India, wracked by sectarian strife, must hold together its democratic framework despite Muslim and Hindu extremists. This newly significant struggle within Islam, superimposed on an older Muslim history, will shape political and economic destinies throughout the region and beyond. Hence, the focus of our series.

We hope that these books will enlighten both teacher and student about a critical subject in a critical area of the world. Central Asia and Asia would be important in their own right to Americans; arguably, after 9/11, they became vital to our national security. And the enduring impact of Islam is a crucial factor we must understand. We at the Foreign Policy Research Institute hope these books will illuminate both the facts and the prospects.

Bangladeshi women light candles in remembrance of those who lost their lives in the country's 1971 war of independence from Pakistan.

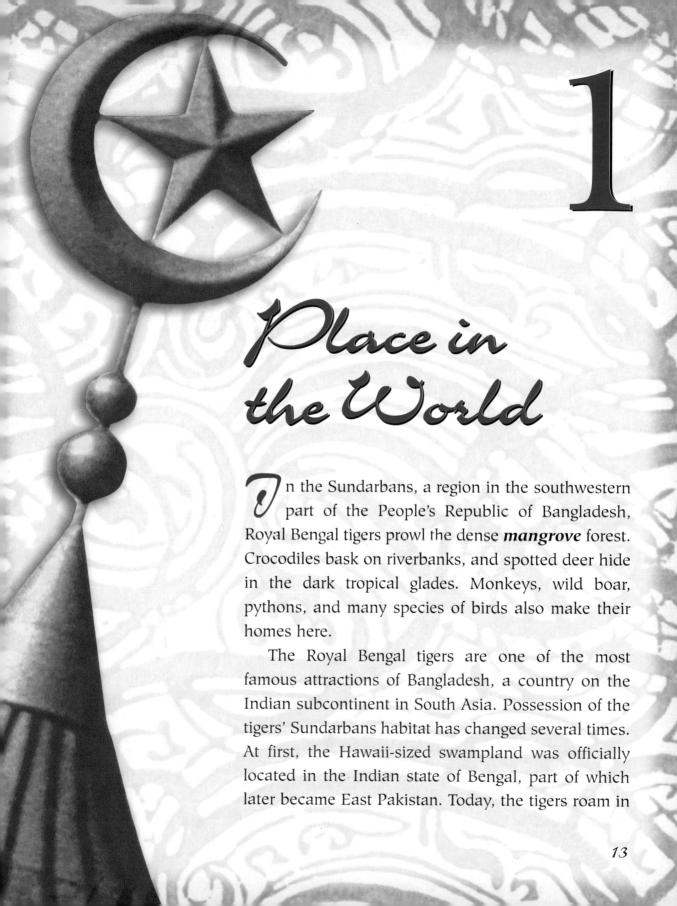

1

Place in the World

In the Sundarbans, a region in the southwestern part of the People's Republic of Bangladesh, Royal Bengal tigers prowl the dense **mangrove** forest. Crocodiles bask on riverbanks, and spotted deer hide in the dark tropical glades. Monkeys, wild boar, pythons, and many species of birds also make their homes here.

The Royal Bengal tigers are one of the most famous attractions of Bangladesh, a country on the Indian subcontinent in South Asia. Possession of the tigers' Sundarbans habitat has changed several times. At first, the Hawaii-sized swampland was officially located in the Indian state of Bengal, part of which later became East Pakistan. Today, the tigers roam in two regions—West Bengal in India and Bangladesh, which has been an independent republic since 1971.

Until 1947 Bangladesh was known as East Bengal—the eastern section of the Indian state of Bengal. That year, just before the British pulled out of India after almost 200 years of rule, they separated the northwest section of the country and added to it East Bengal, forming a new nation named Pakistan.

About 1,000 miles (1,609 km) of Indian territory stood between the two parts of this new nation, West and East Pakistan. The citizens of West Pakistan, formerly the northwestern part of India, were overwhelmingly Muslim. While East Pakistan (formerly East Bengal) had a Muslim majority, Hindus and Buddhists constituted a significant proportion of the population. At the time of independence in 1947, Hindus alone accounted for as many as one in three residents of East Pakistan.

In many respects the people of East Pakistan, who called themselves Bengalis, were treated like second-class citizens. Although the majority spoke the Bangla language, some West Pakistanis sought to ban that tongue and demanded that Urdu become the official language of East Pakistan. The language issue and economic disputes festered until a civil war erupted in 1971. Nine months later, East Pakistan claimed its independence. In naming the country, the Bengalis emphasized their language and heritage by combining two words, *Bangla* and *Desh*. Together, the words mean "land where the Bangla language is spoken."

Bangladesh is only about the size of Wisconsin, but its population is almost half that of the entire United States. In fact, it is the world's most densely populated country that is not an island.

Bangladesh is crisscrossed with mighty rivers and tributaries that empty into the Bay of Bengal. India's great river, the sacred Ganges, flows southeast into Bangladesh. Another major river, the Brahmaputra, enters Bangladesh from the north and flows through the center of the country as the Jamuna River. The Ganges and Jamuna unite to form the Padma River, which is joined below Bangladesh's capital, Dhaka, by the Meghna. At the point where these rivers and their numerous tributaries run into the Bay of Bengal, they deposit **silt** to form a **delta**. This delta at the Mouths of the Ganges is the largest in the world, covering an area of roughly 30,000 squares miles (75,000 sq km).

A Land of Turmoil and Hope

For the people of Bangladesh, the rivers are a blessing but also, to a certain degree, a curse. While the rivers provide livelihoods for fishermen and rich soil for farmers, they also bring widespread destruction. The people of Bangladesh divide their year into six seasons, which pass from heavy monsoons to severe droughts. The season of *barsa*, which takes place from June to October, brings heavy rains that cause extensive flooding. Storms arising in the Bay of Bengal prevent the floodwaters from draining. Sometimes **cyclones** arrive toward the end of the monsoon season, often causing severe damage and many deaths.

Poverty is another destructive force affecting many Bangladeshis. Although some have prospered since the country gained its independence, about 35 percent of Bangladesh's people live below the official poverty line. Bangladesh is largely a nation of subsistence farmers.

The Bangladeshi government has experienced many political storms. The country was founded as a parliamentary democracy under a constitution; however, this ideal form of government did not last. Political corruption, assassination, and turmoil marked Bangladesh's first decades. And, it seems, corruption has remained a constant in the early years of the 21st century.

Through all the political turmoil and the enduring poverty of its people, however, Bangladesh remains a country founded on hope. Not long after independence, Muhammad Yunus, a Bangladeshi economics professor at

The Royal Bengal tiger, which roams southwestern Bangladesh's Sundarbans region, is one of the country's most famous attractions. This specimen was photographed in Dhaka's zoo.

Chittagong University, pioneered a way to help destitute people improve their situation. Yunus founded the Grameen Bank, one of the world's first micro-credit banks. Unlike typical banks, micro-credit banks offer loans to poor people—particularly in rural areas—who otherwise would not qualify for credit. The recipients of these small loans, who are usually women, believe that they can rise above the scarcity threatening their lives and the lives of their children. In many places in Bangladesh, hope survives. It is a force as mighty as the country's raging rivers.

The streets of Bangladesh's capital, Dhaka, were turned into canals during severe flooding in July and August of 2004. A low-lying land that is crisscrossed by rivers, Bangladesh suffers regular floods.

2

The Land

angladesh is a maze of rivers that cut through low-lying flat land. Forests cover these plains and the low hills in the northeast and southeast districts. The country, which has a total area of 55,598 square miles (144,000 sq km), is located on the northeastern side of the South Asian subcontinent. India bounds Bangladesh on the east, west, and north. Burma (also known as Myanmar) borders Bangladesh on the southeast. The southern border is formed by the Bay of Bengal, which Bangladesh shares with India and Burma.

Although Nepal does not border Bangladesh (the Indian state of West Bengal divides the two nations), its major landmark, Mount Everest, towers over the mighty Himalayan Mountains a mere 100 miles (161 km) from the northwestern tip of Bangladesh. Nepal and Bangladesh nearly split the bulk of India from its easternmost states, with a strip of land only 18 miles (29 km) wide connecting the two sections of the country.

The Rivers

A significant portion of Bangladesh's landscape consists of the network of rivers that empties into the Bay of Bengal at the Mouths of the Ganges. Bangladesh sits on the eastern section of the Ganges Plain, a delta region formed by three major rivers—the Ganges, Brahmaputra, and Meghna—and their tributaries. The Ganges River rises along the southern slopes of the Himalayan Mountains in India and flows southeast through Bangladesh. The Brahmaputra River begins on the northern slopes of the Himalayas, flows down through China into India, and crosses into Bangladesh, where it becomes the Jamuna River. The third major river system, the Meghna, rises in northeastern Bangladesh.

The nutrient-rich silt that flows down these rivers builds up on the riverbanks and creates a huge floodplain made up of **sediment** called **alluvium**. Most of Bangladesh consists of this material, which forms a flat, low-lying plain of sand and soil and is good for agriculture. Except for the hilly areas in the far northeast and southeast, the country lies at an elevation of 50 feet (15 meters) or less above sea level.

Bangladesh's great rivers dominate the economic and cultural life of the country. During the rainy season, about one-third of the land is flooded. The high silt content of the floodwaters continually revitalizes farmland. When the rivers overflow during the rainy season, their muddy waters leave behind alluvium rich in nutrients. Rice and jute (a fiber used to make rope, burlap, and carpet backing) thrive in this wet, delta environment. Bangladeshi farmers also grow wheat, sugarcane, and vegetables in the rich delta soil. About two-thirds of Bangladesh's land is used for the cultivation of crops, according to a 2001 estimate (by comparison, the figure is less than 20 percent in the United States).

The Geography of Bangladesh

Location: Southern Asia, bordering the Bay of Bengal,
between Burma and India
Area: (about the size of Wisconsin)
  total: 55,598 square miles (144,000 sq km)
  land: 51,703 square miles (133,910 sq km)
  water: 3,895 square miles (10,090 sq km)
Borders: Burma, 311 miles (193 km); India, 2,518 miles
  (4,053 km)
Climate: tropical; mild winter (October to March); hot,
  humid summer (March to June); humid, warm rainy
  monsoon (June to October)
Terrain: mostly flat alluvial plain; hilly in southeast
Elevation extremes:
  lowest point: Indian Ocean, 0 feet
  highest point: Keokradong, 4,035 feet (1,230 meters)
Natural hazards: droughts, cyclones, tornadoes; much of
  country routinely inundated during monsoon season

Source: Adapted from CIA World Factbook, 2004.

The Hills

The land in Bangladesh that is not river delta land consists mostly of low hills, tropical jungles, and marshy swamps. Rolling hills covered with green forests rise in the far northeast Sylhet Division and in the southeast corners of the Chittagong Division. (The six divisions of Bangladesh, which are similar to U.S. states, are composed of smaller districts.) Most of Bangladesh's hills range from about 800 feet (244 meters) high in the north to about 200 feet (61 meters) high in the south. The Chittagong Hills in the Chittagong Division form the highest and most rugged area of the country. These hills are part of rolling, forested regions known as the Chittagong Hill Tracts.

There are three districts within the Chittagong Hill Tracts: Rangamati, Khagrachari, and Banderban. Together, they contain seven river valleys spanning 5,093 square miles (13,295 sq km), or 10 percent of the total land area of Bangladesh. With its ravines and cliffs shrouded in dense vegetation, this region stands in sharp contrast to the alluvial plain that dominates the rest of the country.

The Chittagong Hill Tracts borders the Indian states of Tripura on the north and Mizoram on the east. Burma sits on the south and east, and on the west are the districts of Chittagong and Cox's Bazar. This narrow coastal strip is the only region where river deltas do not break up the land. Near the Burma border stands Mount Keokradong, which at 4,035 feet (1,230 meters) above sea level is the country's highest peak.

Green rolling hills mark the Sylhet Division of northeast Bangladesh. Thick tropical forests and scenic, terraced tea plantations dot this region of the country. The Sylhet Division's Surma River valley contains wooded marshes and dense jungles that add to the area's lush beauty. The valley has many *haors*, large natural depressions in the land. In the winter these depressions are covered with green vegetation and provide homes for many migratory birds; during the rainy season, however, they fill with water that is sometimes quite turbulent.

Bangladesh's hills, mountains, and valleys contain few of the rock formations that in neighboring countries often form steep mountain terrain. In fact, rocks are almost nonexistent in Bangladesh, whose hills are made of sand and a clay-like soil that is easily formed into bricks.

"The Beautiful Forest"

About 15 percent of Bangladesh consists of woodlands and forest, and one of the world's most extraordinary natural ecosystems, the

This view from the Chittagong Division in eastern Bangladesh shows a mosaic of rice paddies.

Sundarbans, lies along the southwest corner of the Bay of Bengal coastline. The name *Sundarban* comes from a Bengali word that means "the Beautiful Forest." This densely wooded tidal area is shared between India and Bangladesh. A protected ecosystem, it has been declared a Natural World Heritage site in both countries.

This tropical forest is a cluster of 200 islands separated and interconnected by 400 tidal rivers, creeks, and canals along the Bay of Bengal. The Sundarbans covers approximately 3,860 square miles (10,000 sq km) of land and water. Sixty-two percent, or nearly 2,400 square miles (6,000 sq km), of the Sundarbans rests in Bangladesh in the Khulna Division.

In the Sundarbans, forest and river collide. The region houses the world's largest mangrove forest; these tropical trees, which form dense thickets in the swamps, have tree roots that grow down from the branches instead of growing from the trunk. The Sundarbans is also home to thousands of wild animals—48 species of mammals, 315 species of birds, 53 species of reptiles (including crocodiles and cobras), and 120 species of fish. The most famous inhabitants, however, are the Royal Bengal tigers.

Climate

Bangladesh has one of the wettest climates in the world, and for most of the year, heat and humidity nurture the lush vegetation along the rivers. During the winter months, the cooling influence of the Himalayas and the Bay of Bengal reduces the temperatures and humidity. Bangladesh lies in the subtropical monsoon region to the south of the Himalayas, a location that makes it one of the most flood-prone countries in the world. When the mountain snow melts, the Ganges and Brahmaputra Rivers and their tributaries carry the runoff to the Bay of Bengal. As the rivers become swollen with snowmelt and copious rainfall, much of Bangladesh floods.

Heavy rains occur during the monsoon season, which runs from June to October. Most regions receive between 60 and 100 inches (152 and 254 centimeters) of rain annually. Some areas in the northeast and southeast near the hills receive more than 200 inches (508 cm) of rain a year.

Between October and March, weather conditions are more moderate. Heavy rains and sticky heat give way to relatively mild temperatures. January is usually the coolest month, with an average temperature of about 50° Fahrenheit (10° Celsius). This dry season during the winter months is a welcome respite from the monsoons.

In Bangladesh, the hottest month is May, when the average temperature climbs to about 82°F (28°C). June marks the beginning of the rainy

The monsoon season, which runs from June to October, brings heavy rains and, in many years, widespread flooding.

season. By the middle of the month, the Bangladeshis have suffered storms called nor'westers that pack high winds and drop torrential rains.

Toward the end of the monsoon season, cyclones strike the country, particularly the coastal districts along the Bay of Bengal. These intense tropical storms bring extremely high winds and heavy rains. Often the winds, which reach speeds of 100–150 miles (160–241 km) per hour, push deadly tidal waves out of the Bay of Bengal. Rising as high as 20 feet (6 meters), these waves crash with tremendous force onto the coastal lands and offshore islands. The storms that hit Bangladesh often destroy villages and towns and kill thousands of people in their path.

More than 50 cyclones have struck the Bangladesh coast since 1900, causing hundreds of thousands of deaths and untold misery. In November

1970 more than a quarter million people perished in a devastating cyclone along the central shores of the Bay of Bengal. This storm not only devastated lives and property but also had grave political consequences. Bengalis felt that the national government in West Pakistan did not do enough to help them recover from the terrible storm, and this grievance was a factor in the independence movement that led to the founding of Bangladesh the following year. Two decades later, in April 1991, the young country of Bangladesh suffered another devastating cyclone that took some 140,000 lives.

Sometimes farmers welcome the floodwaters; other times they despair over them. Flooded rivers may rise 10 feet (3 meters) above their banks in low-lying areas. If the floods gently cover the lowlands, large quantities of nutrient-rich silt are deposited. And if the monsoon comes on time, the

Over the years, cyclones have exacted a terrible toll on Bangladesh—in some cases, hundreds of thousands have been killed by a single storm. Here residents survey the ruins of Kamarpara, a village north of Dhaka that was destroyed by a cyclone's fierce winds.

enriched soil left behind by the rivers, along with the water supplied by the heavy rains, allows rice to be grown and harvested three times during the year. If, however, the floodwaters are too swift, they damage the crops in their wake. On these occasions, farmers may lose 10 to 20 percent of their crop yields.

If rains come too late, people can suffer even more. Without the needed rain, crops fail and hunger, always a problem in this overpopulated country, reaches widespread proportions.

Natural Resources

Natural gas has been discovered recently in Bangladesh, and some oil companies are considering investments in oil and natural gas exploration in the country. Unfortunately, no other commercially significant mineral has been discovered in quantities sufficient to allow exportation. Deposits of coal, limestone, and peat exist, but they are not large enough to be of much value.

Forests constitute another of Bangladesh's natural resources. Wood comes from three principal regions: the Sundarbans along the coast, the Madhupur jungle, and the Chittagong Hills. Bamboo and rattan are abundant. Mango, palm, and tamarind trees grow throughout most of the country. Teak grows in the tropical rain forest of the Chittagong Hills.

The fertile soil produced by the river sediment remains the country's chief resource. In almost all parts of the country, farmers tend the rich soil to grow rice, jute, tobacco, sugarcane, **pulses** (lentils and other **legumes**), and wheat. The rivers that dominate the lives of the Bangladeshis bring with them the blessings of bountiful harvests and the curse of floods. Many people cultivate and live on flood-prone land that is often polluted. The water from these mighty rivers and their many tributaries is equally dangerous as a source of various diseases.

This painting depicts a scene from the Mahabharata. The Hindu epic, believed to have been composed between 200 B.C. and A.D. 200, contains one of the first-known references to Vanga, an early kingdom in the land of present-day Bangladesh.

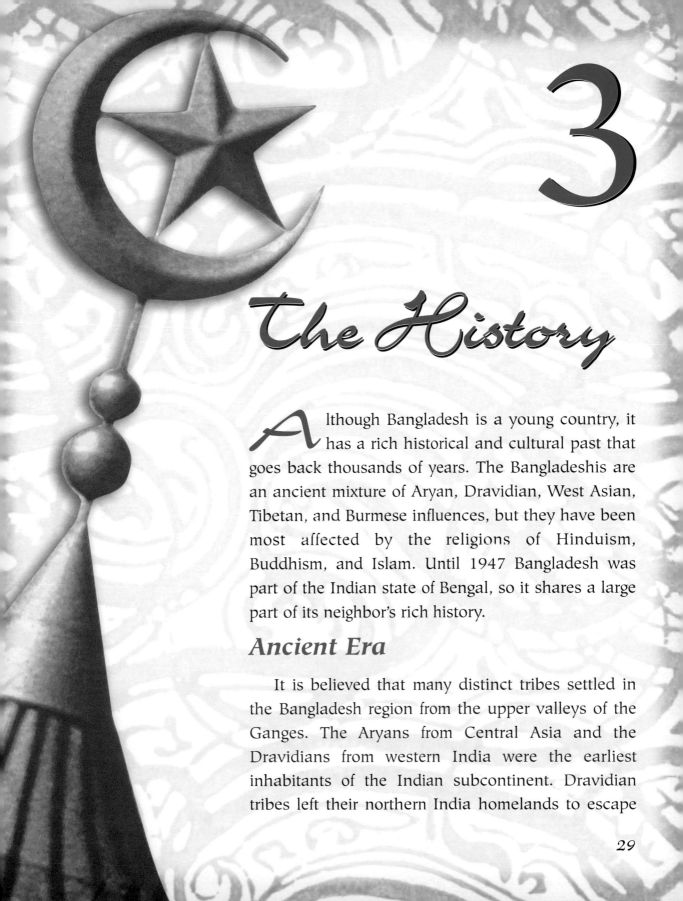

3

The History

Although Bangladesh is a young country, it has a rich historical and cultural past that goes back thousands of years. The Bangladeshis are an ancient mixture of Aryan, Dravidian, West Asian, Tibetan, and Burmese influences, but they have been most affected by the religions of Hinduism, Buddhism, and Islam. Until 1947 Bangladesh was part of the Indian state of Bengal, so it shares a large part of its neighbor's rich history.

Ancient Era

It is believed that many distinct tribes settled in the Bangladesh region from the upper valleys of the Ganges. The Aryans from Central Asia and the Dravidians from western India were the earliest inhabitants of the Indian subcontinent. Dravidian tribes left their northern India homelands to escape

Indo-Aryan control. Later, Indo-Aryan tribes pushed into the Dravidian areas. Among these migrating tribes was a group called the Bang, from whom modern Bangladesh takes its name. At the time these tribes settled, the land area was much smaller. Since then, 3,000 years of river deposits have enlarged the delta.

The Mahabharata, a Hindu epic whose composition many scholars date to between 200 B.C. and A.D. 200, contains one of the first-known references to Vanga, an obscure kingdom that flourished earlier in Bengal, on territory that now forms part of Bangladesh. Not much is known about Vanga, except that it was subsumed by the Mauryan Empire in the third century B.C.

The Mauryan Empire

The Mauryan Empire was the first of the great empires to sweep across India, and the first to create a single government for the whole region. Bengal was its easternmost outpost. From about 321 to 185 B.C., Mauryan emperors ruled from their center in Magadha, a rich kingdom in the Ganges Valley. It was during this period that Buddhism, a religion that had been founded by Siddhartha Gautama (ca. 563–ca. 483 B.C.), was spread throughout the Indian subcontinent, including Bengal.

India and its surrounding territories prospered during Mauryan rule. The government developed and owned all agricultural lands, forests, mines, and craft works. Public irrigation helped farmers produce rich harvests. Many of the crops—rice, wheat, barley, cotton, vegetables, and pulses—are still cultivated today.

The Gupta Empire

Little record survives of the period after the decline of the Mauryan Empire until the fourth century A.D. From about A.D. 320 to 550, Bengal was part of the Gupta Empire, which encompassed much of northern India and was ruled by members of the powerful Gupta family.

The Gupta period saw many advances in the fields of literature, sculpture, and other fine arts. Most Gupta emperors were Hindus, but Buddhism also thrived under their rule, as did Jainism, a third major religion founded in India. Many Hindu social and religious practices were formalized during this time, and the images of Hindu gods and goddesses became objects of worship.

Sanskrit, the classical Indian language, flourished during the Gupta dynasty. Hindu schools and Buddhist monasteries taught subjects that are still popular today, such as astronomy, grammar, mathematics, medicine, philosophy, and religion. In fact, Gupta Empire mathematicians invented the decimal systems and the Hindu-Arabic numerals that are still used today all over the world.

The Gupta emperors left Bengal alone as long as the local chieftains paid their taxes. The delta area became the kingdom of Samatata, centered near the present-day city of Chandpur in the southern half of the Chittagong Division. But Bengal essentially remained a backwater region that went forgotten most of the time.

Pala and Sena Dynasties

During the middle of the eighth century, Buddhist rulers gained control of eastern Bengal, and Buddhist culture spread throughout the region for the next 300 years. The Palas—the designation

An inscribed iron pillar from the Gupta Empire, which held sway over Bengal between the early fourth and mid-sixth centuries.

comes from the rulers' practice of attaching the suffix *-pala*, meaning "protector," to their names—became one of three dynastic families controlling the Indian subcontinent. Devout Buddhists, the Palas founded many monasteries and Buddhist schools.

Buddhism was popular among the poorer classes because its social values were relatively democratic. By contrast, Hinduism dictated a rigid **caste** system, dividing the population (from birth) along sharply defined social lines that individuals could never transcend. Those from the higher castes enjoyed wealth, status, power, and respect; those from the lowest castes led lives of poverty and, frequently, endured scorn and mistreatment. Later, beginning in the early 13th century, Islam would have an appeal mirroring that of Buddhism, for similar reasons.

When the Pala dynasty weakened, the Senas gained power around the middle of the 11th century. Because the Senas were orthodox Hindus, they immediately reinstated the caste system, but in Bengal, they introduced *kulinism*, a Hindu social code that allowed certain men from the highest caste to marry women from the caste below, but prohibited women from marrying below their caste. Although kulinism enabled some families to improve their status through a daughter's marriage, it also encouraged polygamy, as high-caste men often took many wives simply to collect their dowries. And the lower classes continued to suffer under the caste system's prohibitions.

The Rise of Islam

During the eighth century Arab Muslims began invading the region that would become Pakistan. These invaders championed their religion, which at that time was barely 100 years old. Islam, based on the teachings of its founder and prophet, Muhammad, had originated in the Arabian Peninsula.

Three hundred years later a Turkish ruler named Mahmud of Ghazni established a kingdom in the Pakistan region. This was the first Muslim

By the turn of the 13th century, Bengal had been incorporated into the Muslim empire known as the Delhi Sultanate. Islam's influence on Bangladesh has been profound.

state on the Indian subcontinent. In 1199 Mohammed Bakhtiar captured Bengal and incorporated the region into the Muslim empire called the Delhi Sultanate (a sultanate is a kingdom controlled by a Muslim ruler known as a sultan). By 1206 most of northern India was part of the Delhi Sultanate.

In 1341 Bengal gained its independence from the Delhi Sultanate. From that year until 1576, independent Muslim rulers governed parts of Bengal and its neighboring states.

Mughal Rule

In 1576 the Muslim emperor Akbar (1542–1605) sent his armies east to conquer the rich province of Bengal. Akbar, one of the greatest rulers in the history of India, already had extended his domain over most of Afghanistan, India, and Pakistan; now he added Bengal. He was the most skilled of the Mughal emperors, who were descendants of the Mongols hailing from the **steppes** of Central Asia. Over the next two centuries, Mughal emperors controlled much of the Indian subcontinent, and under their rule most of East Bengal converted to Islam. In 1608 Akbar's successor, his son Jahangir, established the Mughal capital at the Bengal city of Dhaka. The city would maintain an important role for the rest of the empire's history.

The Mughal period was one of the most stable times in India's history. The emperors instituted a system of governors called **nawabs**. These appointed officials, who ruled the provinces of the empire (a practice that continued into modern times), grew increasingly powerful as Bengal and other provinces became more independent. Finally, in the early 1700s, the Mughal Empire began to break up.

The Coming of the Europeans

The Mughals were not the only people to dominate Bengal. During the two centuries that the Mughals influenced Bengali language, food, dress, and customs, European traders from Portugal, the Netherlands, France, and Great Britain were building trade routes and allying themselves with the powerful nawabs. In the 1500s European outposts were set up and began competing for the profitable trade between the East Indies and Europe.

By the turn of the 17th century, European countries such as England, the Netherlands, France, and Denmark began establishing East India companies. These private enterprises, chartered by their respective governments, were given special rights to trade with India and the Far East.

The British East India Company, founded in 1600, would outlast its rivals and remain involved in trade in India for more than 200 years. In fact, the company was the driving force behind India's incorporation into the British Empire. By the mid-1600s the British East India Company was operating a jute-processing factory in Bengal; in the last decade of the century the company established an important trade center and fort in Calcutta, on the eastern coast of present-day India. The British East India Company secured its trade position by insinuating itself into local politics and, when necessary, using its own private army to fend off hostile rulers or European rivals such as the French.

As the British East India Company gained more control, the Mughal Empire dissolved. In 1757 the British East India Company finally solidified its authority when the last Muslim nawab of Bengal was defeated at the Battle of Plassey by British East India Company forces under the command of Robert Clive. Clive then set up a new nawab that he and the company could control. From that time onward, a succession of company officials effectively ruled most of Bengal.

Commanding the military forces of the British East India Company, Robert Clive defeated the Muslim nawab of Bengal at the Battle of Plassey. That 1757 victory solidified British influence on the Indian subcontinent.

The British East India Company made huge profits on jute production in East Bengal, though the Bengalis did not benefit from this revenue. Despite their valuable contributions as factory workers and as soldiers, they were treated as inferiors.

In 1857 a revolt by Indian soldiers, known as sepoys, broke out against the British. The Sepoy Rebellion, also known as the Indian Rebellion, failed. But the British government, recognizing the seriousness of the threat to a prized imperial possession, moved in 1858 to abolish the East India Company and transfer direct authority for administering Bengal and the other Indian territories to the British crown.

The British Raj

The rule of Great Britain over India is often called the British Raj. *Raja* is a Hindu term for a member of the nobility, and the officials who governed India were high-ranking English noblemen. Because India became known as the crown jewel of the British Empire, the aristocrats considered a government position in India a prize assignment.

During the British administration, the western region of Bengal experienced industrial and cultural growth. The eastern region did not fare as well. While the city of Calcutta became a hub of the British Empire, Dhaka in eastern Bengal faded in importance, its status slipping from regional capital to district headquarters. Although farmers of the region still produced much of the jute that was sent to Britain and other international markets, the profitable jute-processing factories were set up in Calcutta. Similarly, while the people of eastern Bengal supplied much of the food and raw materials for the west, they did not enjoy a significant share in the profits.

Overall, Hindus more easily accepted British rule than did Muslims. For decades only British were accepted into the civil service or permitted to work in high-status fields such as medicine and law. As these restrictions were relaxed somewhat around the turn of the 20th century, those Indians who did win good positions were mostly Hindus. Muslims, meanwhile, tended to remain farmers and laborers. This disparity caused such discontent between the Hindus and Muslims that in 1905 the British divided Bengal into two parts, West Bengal and East Bengal, respectively composed of Hindu and Muslim majorities.

The partition of Bengal was not a successful move. Fearing a restriction of their profitable commercial interests and a loss of seats in the provincial legislature that the British had established, Bengali Hindus staged many protests and refused to buy British goods. Prominent Hindu landowners, professional groups, and tradesmen viewed the partition as a threat to their political and economic power. However, Bengali Muslims supported the separation because they hoped to gain economic and political opportunities. Upon realizing that the Muslim-Hindu problem would not be resolved, the British reunited Bengal in 1911, only six years after the state had been partitioned.

During the short period of partition, the Muslims saw that they could improve their situation and were sparked to action. As one-fifth of the Indian population, they believed that they deserved a greater role. Prominent Muslims doubted that high-ranking Hindus would heed their interests, so they formed the Muslim League in 1906. This party grew increasingly powerful in the 1930s and 1940s as its members petitioned for a separate Muslim state.

During this time, the British faced mounting pressure for Indian independence. However, as the momentum built for an independent India, so did the demand for a separate Muslim state. In the legislative elections of 1945–1946, the Muslim League—the main proponent of a separate homeland for Muslims—won a huge landslide in districts reserved for Muslim representatives, which bolstered its demands.

In July of 1947, Britain's Parliament passed the India Independence Act, which specified the partition of British India into two countries, one of which, Pakistan, would include a majority Muslim population. On August 15, 1947, British rule in India ceased, and the independent nations of India and Pakistan officially came into existence.

In earlier referendums, the provinces of British India had decided which country they would belong to. The western Muslim districts had voted to become part of Pakistan, as had the districts of East Bengal. With these regions so far apart, leaders decided to establish West and East Pakistan, two entities of a single state. West Pakistan would have four provinces, while East Pakistan, formerly East Bengal, would consist of a single province with its capital at Dhaka. Each province would have a legislature and elected leaders serving in the national parliament.

Lord Mountbatten, the British viceroy of India, formally announces the end of British rule in India, August 15, 1947. That day, two independent states came into existence: India and Pakistan.

But this arrangement—and indeed, the partition of British India itself—did not solve all of the region's religious and ethnic problems. Even before the actual partition, horrendous violence erupted between Hindu and Muslim communities. Massacres and reprisals claimed the lives of countless people, and millions of refugees were created. Desperate Muslims in the new Indian state of Punjab streamed across the border into Pakistan, and fearful Hindus abandoned their homes in the Pakistani territories and fled to India. And all the while the killing continued. Ultimately the death toll reached about one million, according to most estimates.

In addition to the intercommunal violence that exploded with the creation of independent India and Pakistan, partition created intractable political problems between the two countries. The princely state of Jammu and Kashmir, in northwest India, had a Muslim majority that wanted to become a part of Pakistan, yet its ruler was a Hindu with allegiances to India. Pakistan and India fought the First Kashmir War in 1947 over the issue. Eventually, India took control of most of the region, though ownership remains contested today, and Pakistan has been accused of supporting Muslim **insurgents** in Kashmir.

East Pakistan

Independent Pakistan was barely two years old before trouble began in East Pakistan, and over the next two decades the problems only worsened. Political instability and economic difficulties marked the development of Pakistan. Although the government strove to maintain a civilian leadership that was held accountable by a parliament and a constitution, the military often proved to have a stronger influence. It declared **martial law** and controlled the country between 1958 and 1962, and again between 1969 and 1972.

Furthermore, although the citizens of East Pakistan had been some of the strongest supporters of a Muslim state, they did not want to be under the thumb of the stronger, more affluent West Pakistan. A number of issues divided the two halves of Pakistan. East Pakistan remained the less developed wing of the new nation, and its people believed that the Pakistani government (which was located in West Pakistan) did little to improve their economy and living conditions. As one of the world's major producers of jute, East Pakistan felt that it deserved a fairer share of the trade profits. As they had experienced under the British, East Pakistanis believed they were being exploited for the valuable **commodity**.

Along with resenting this economic imbalance, the East Pakistanis (or Bengalis, as they preferred to be called) took issue with West Pakistan's overbearing role in East Pakistan's administration. Because Muslim Bengalis had a general lack of administrative experience, many West Pakistanis were brought in to fill the high-ranking positions left vacant when Hindu Bengalis fled to India after the partition. In the civil service as well as in the military, Bengalis were underrepresented.

However, the issue that most sharply divided East and West was language. The West Pakistani government wanted to establish Urdu as the official language of the nation, even though Bangla was the common language of East Pakistan. The issue reached a breaking point on February 21, 1952, when students and others marched in protest against the government proposal to make Urdu the official language. While the National Assembly was debating the issue in Karachi, then the capital of Pakistan, demonstrators took to the streets in Dhaka. Police fired on the marchers, killing several students. (February 21 has since become Martyr's Day in Bangladesh, honoring the students of the Language Movement who died defending Bengali culture.) The conflict finally was resolved in September 1954 when the Pakistani government agreed to establish both Urdu and Bangla as the official languages of the country.

With the goal of gaining autonomy for East Pakistan, the Awami Muslim League (later shortened to the Awami League) had formed in

1949. In the elections of 1954, the Awami League stood as the main rival of the West Pakistani–controlled Muslim League, and it became a leading voice for Bengali causes. Unlike the exclusively Islamic Muslim League, the Awami League admitted Hindus and other minorities. One of the leaders of this new party was a Bengali named Sheikh Mujibur Rahman, popularly known as Sheikh Mujib. He and other prominent Awami League members soon became major forces in the Bengali drive for independence.

In 1966 Sheikh Mujib presented a six-point plan for East Pakistan self-rule, for which he was labeled a security threat and put in prison.

By 1971 disputes between East and West Pakistan had boiled over. This round of troubles began in November 1970 after a devastating cyclone struck East Pakistan, killing about 266,000 Bengalis. Relief was slow to come, and many Bengalis accused the government of delaying shipments and relief supplies.

A month after the cyclone hit, national elections exacerbated the tensions. These elections—which were particularly important because the National Assembly was planning to draft a new constitution—resulted in the Awami League's gaining 167 of the 313 seats in Pakistan's legislature. Sheikh Mujib (released from jail in 1969) had

Sheikh Mujibur Rahman, an early champion of self-rule for East Pakistan, served as independent Bangladesh's first prime minister. But he soon took on dictatorial powers and, in 1975, was killed in a coup.

Sheikh Mujibur Rahman

Sheikh Mujibur Rahman was the first president and prime minister of Bangladesh. Politically active throughout his adult life, Rahman was a fearless supporter of Bengali interests. In 1966 he announced a six-point program for East Pakistan self-rule. This program became the foundation of Bengali independence. Today the Bengali word *Bangabandhu*, meaning "friend of the Bengalis," is attached to his name. Although his administration ended prematurely with his assassination, today Rahman is considered the father and political architect of his country.

campaigned for greater self-government for East Pakistan, and the Bengalis had responded. For several months after the elections, representatives of the Pakistan People's Party and the Awami League, led by Rahman, attempted to reach an agreement on the issue of self-government. Ultimately, however, the talks proved fruitless.

On March 25, 1971, Pakistan's president, Yahya Khan, sent troops to put down Bengali protests. Rahman was arrested and the Awami League banned. The next day, East Pakistan declared its independence, proclaiming the new nation Bangladesh. This signaled the beginning of what became known as the War of Liberation, which would last for nine months.

Many of Rahman's aides escaped to India and established a provisional government there; they were eventually joined by more than 10 million Bengali refugees. A guerrilla army known as the Mukti Bahini was all Bangladesh had standing against the stronger, better-prepared Pakistani national army.

In the early days of the conflict, the Pakistanis organized a terror campaign, concentrating a brutal offensive on Dhaka. By the summer of 1971 an estimated 300,000 Bangladeshis had already been killed. But the flood of Bangladeshi refugees, along with international pressure to do something about the attacks on its essentially defenseless neighbor, pulled India into the conflict. In June, Indian army officers began training the Mukti Bahini and strengthening its forces along the East Pakistan borders. In November, India officially declared war on Pakistan.

India's entry into the conflict proved decisive. Pakistani forces were soon in retreat, and on December 16, 1971, they officially surrendered to the Indian army. The People's Republic of Bangladesh was born.

A New Nation

Mujibur Rahman returned to his newly independent country to take command. At first he was tremendously popular, but he had difficulty establishing a stable political foundation, a problem that would plague Bangladesh for many years.

By November 1972 Bangladesh had drafted a constitution, which became effective the following month. The constitution established a parliamentary democracy that basically followed the British model, except that Bangladesh's parliament, the Jatiya Sangsad, had one house instead of two. The executive branch consisted of a prime minister as well as a president, whose position was largely ceremonial. An independent court system was also established.

In the first years after independence, no other political party rose to challenge the dominance of the Awami League. The ruling party established a socialist economic system, nationalizing about 85 percent of Bangladesh's industries, such as the jute and cotton textile plants and the sugar mills. Putting the nation's industries under government control is a cornerstone of a socialist system, but such a system requires experienced and competent managers, which Bangladesh largely lacked. In addition, corruption among those in positions of authority began to proliferate.

Despite this corruption, along with a fair degree of social and political unrest, Bangladesh's parliamentary system plodded along for two years, with Mujibur Rahman running the government as prime minister. In December 1974, however, Rahman declared a state of emergency and suspended fundamental rights, including those granted in the constitution. A month later, the constitution was amended, and the parliamentary system disappeared. Rahman named himself president, and rather than sharing power with an elected parliament, he ran the country as a virtual dictator.

In June 1975 the Bangladesh Krishak Sramik Awami League (BAKSAL), under the leadership of Rahman, was named the only legal political party in the country. BAKSAL drafted a new constitution to correspond with its political views. Two months later Rahman was assassinated in a military **coup** known as the "majors' plot." The group of officers behind the assassination designated Khondakar Mushtaque Ahmed as president. Ahmed, who promised new elections and a return to the parliamentary system, immediately abolished BAKSAL.

The Ahmed government did not last long. In November 1975 another military coup ousted Ahmed and brought A. S. M. Sayem to power as president and chief martial law administrator (CMLA), a new designation for the head of the government during the political crisis (the constitution remained suspended).

Soon, Major General Ziaur Rahman emerged as a leading figure in national politics. The following November, Ziaur Rahman, popularly known as Zia, became the CMLA. In April 1976 Zia consolidated his power after President Sayem's resignation on the dubious grounds of "poor health." In 1977 he became Bangladesh's president.

Zia gradually returned Bangladesh to democracy. In 1979 multiparty elections were held, with Zia winning election as president, and his

Bangladesh Nationalist Party (BNP) garnering the most seats in the Jatiya Sangsad, Bangladesh's parliament. Martial law was abolished and the constitution reestablished. During Zia's administration, Bangladesh progressed economically and living conditions improved.

Unfortunately, Zia was assassinated on May 30, 1981. The vice president, Justice Abdus Sattar, took charge as acting president, but he was removed the following March in a bloodless coup led by Lieutenant General H. M. Ershad. As the new CMLA, Ershad suspended the constitution and declared martial law, dissolved the Jatiya Sangsad, and abolished political parties. Soon he added president of the council of ministers to his title, concentrating virtually all political power in Bangladesh in his own hands.

Although Ershad ruled in an authoritarian manner, he nevertheless strove, over the next four years, to transfer the country from martial law to civilian rule. In 1986 some political rights, including the right to hold public rallies, were restored; parliamentary elections were held in May of that year. While charges of voting irregularities were leveled and the party Ershad had founded—the Jatiya (People's) Party, or JP—won a majority of seats, the Awami League made a respectable showing. The Jatiya Sangsad soon answered Ershad's call for a revised constitution.

Opposition parties boycotted the presidential elections held in November 1986, however. Running unopposed, Ershad won amid further allegations of fraud.

H. M. Ershad, an army general, seized power in a bloodless coup in March 1982. He ruled Bangladesh until December 1990.

In July 1987, opposition parties united to protest government policies, pushing for an end to military control. They wanted an elected prime minister, not a president who in their view amounted to little more than a military dictator. Ershad declared a state of emergency in November, and in December he dissolved the Jatiya Sangsad. In March of the following year, parliamentary elections were held even though the major opposition parties refused to participate. Ershad's JP party won more than 80 percent of the seats, with three minor political parties and some independent candidates splitting the remainder.

During Ershad's administration, the Jatiya Sangsad passed a number of legislative bills. One included a constitutional amendment naming Islam the state religion. This controversial amendment passed because Ershad's JP party controlled 251 of the 300 seats in the legislature, and the major opposition parties (the Awami League and Bangladesh Nationalist Party) held none. Some student protests on college campuses took place, and non-Islamic minorities feared this amendment might lead to conflicts. Such fears, however, proved unfounded.

By 1990 opposition to Ershad had spread. Political parties, civilian groups, and professional organizations demanded free and fair elections. They refused to accept another state of emergency, the means Ershad had used repeatedly to hold on to power. In December, after several months of general strikes, increased campus protests, and public rallies, Ershad finally resigned, and an interim government took power.

On February 27, 1991, Bangladeshis went to the polls to vote in what may have been the country's freest and fairest parliamentary elections ever. The Bangladesh Nationalist Party (BNP) won a plurality of seats and formed a ***coalition*** government with an Islamic fundamentalist party known as the Jamaat-e-Islami (JI). Begum Khaleda Zia, leader of the BNP and widow of Ziaur Rahman, became Bangladesh's prime minister.

Khaleda Zia would remain in office until 1996. During her tenure, Bangladesh's constitution was amended to restore the principles of the 1972 document; a parliamentary system that placed governing power with the prime minister was once again established. In October 1991, members of the Jatiya Sangsad elected a new president, Abdur Rahman Biswas.

A few months earlier, in April, a severe cyclone had hit the country. With winds of 160 miles (257 km) per hour, the storm cut a wide swath of destruction and claimed 138,000 lives. This was the worst cyclone since the one that had devastated the country in 1970.

By 1994 political storms threatened to rip apart the Zia government. In March a special parliamentary election widely believed to have been fraudulent sparked widespread protests. From December 1994 until November 1995, strikes and general shutdowns designed to pressure the Zia government to step down paralyzed the country. Finally, President Biswas dissolved the parliament and set up a **caretaker government** until new elections could be held.

The national elections took place in June 1996. The Awami League gained the majority of seats, and Sheikh Hasina Wazed, the daughter of Sheikh Mujib Rahman, was sworn in as prime minister. Justice Shahabuddin Ahmed replaced Biswas as president.

In 1998 floods that lasted for more than two months covered two-thirds of the country. Heavy rainfall, combined with peak flows of the major rivers, set up disastrous conditions. However, the Wazed government succeeded in handling the natural disasters, and it survived political turmoil as well. During her administration, the Awami League managed for the first time to complete its five-year tenure as the majority party in the Jatiya Sangsad, despite the opposition's attempts to force early elections.

On October 1, 2001, new elections put into power a coalition of the BNP and three other parties led by Khaleda Zia. Zia was once again sworn

Prime Minister Begum Khaleda Zia, leader of the Bangladesh Nationalist Party, addresses supporters during a 2003 rally.

in as prime minister; barring early elections, she will remain in office until 2006.

In 2002 Iajuddin Ahmed, a Dhaka University professor, was sworn in as president. Ahmed (no relation to Shahabuddin Ahmed) had been an adviser to the 1991 caretaker government as well as an official on government commissions.

Political stability has not come with Bangladesh's independence, but since the 1990s, the parliamentary system, working under the constitution that was restored in 1986 and amended several times thereafter, seems to be working. Experts cite the 2001 elections as a sign of a stronger, more secure political system. Despite allegations of electoral fraud leveled by the Awami League, independent international observers declared the 2001 elections free and fair.

If Bangladesh may have at last achieved a measure of political stability, natural disasters continue to ravage the land and the economy. In 2004 widespread flooding claimed more than 700 lives and left an estimated 10 million people homeless. Because the flooding kept many workers from their jobs, economic production declined.

Bangladeshi farmers at work in a rice paddy. Almost two-thirds of Bangladesh's labor force is involved in agriculture.

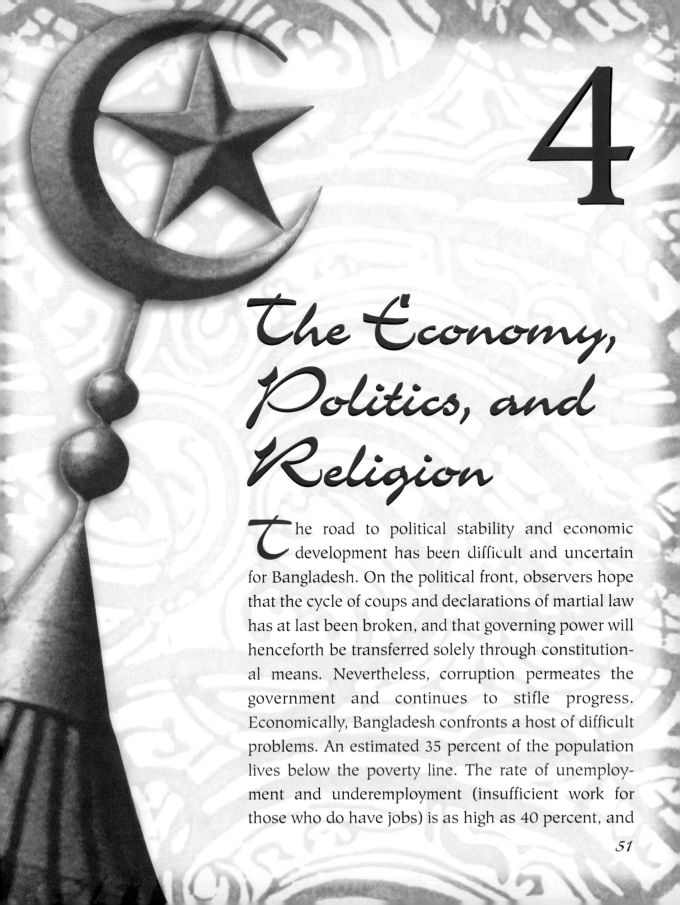

4

The Economy, Politics, and Religion

The road to political stability and economic development has been difficult and uncertain for Bangladesh. On the political front, observers hope that the cycle of coups and declarations of martial law has at last been broken, and that governing power will henceforth be transferred solely through constitutional means. Nevertheless, corruption permeates the government and continues to stifle progress. Economically, Bangladesh confronts a host of difficult problems. An estimated 35 percent of the population lives below the poverty line. The rate of unemployment and underemployment (insufficient work for those who do have jobs) is as high as 40 percent, and

51

Bangladesh's agriculture-based economy is ill-equipped to absorb the demands of a growing labor force.

Economic Overview

Bangladesh is a poor country. Its **gross domestic product (GDP)** for 2004 was estimated at about $259 billion. GDP, which measures the overall size of a national economy and is a primary measure of a country's economic performance, is the total value of goods and services the country produces in a year. Meanwhile, Bangladesh's estimated 2004 GDP per capita was just $1,900. GDP per capita (computed by dividing GDP by population) is each citizen's average share of the country's economic activity and is thus a measure of the economic well-being of a country's people. Bangladesh's GDP per capita is low, falling within the bottom quarter of the world's nations and lagging considerably behind regional neighbors such as India ($2,900) and China ($5,000).

Much of the labor force works outside the country. The Bangladeshis themselves are a major export, providing labor to Saudi Arabia, Kuwait, the United Arab Emirates, Oman, Qatar, and Malaysia. These workers put hundreds of millions of dollars into Bangladesh's economy through remittances from abroad.

Agriculture

Throughout its history, Bangladesh has had a predominantly **agrarian** economy. The agricultural sector accounts for more than 20 percent of the GDP but employs nearly two-thirds (63 percent) of the country's workforce. The fertile soil, replenished annually by silt deposited by the three major rivers, makes up the most important natural resource in Bangladesh.

In the rural areas, Bangladeshis live and work on small farms that average only about 3.5 acres (1.4 hectares). Although modern farming

The Economy of Bangladesh

Gross domestic product (GDP*): $258.8 billion

GDP per capita: $1,900

Natural resources: natural gas, arable land, timber, coal

Industry (26.6% of GDP): cotton textiles, jute, garments, tea processing, paper newsprint, cement, chemical fertilizer, light engineering, sugar

Agriculture (21.7% of GDP): rice, jute, tea, wheat, sugarcane, potatoes, tobacco, pulses, oilseeds, spices, fruit, beef, milk, poultry

Services (51.7% of GDP): transportation, communications, shipping, tourism

Foreign trade:

Imports—$9.459 billion: machinery and equipment, chemicals, iron and steel, textiles, foodstuffs, petroleum products, cement (2003 est.)

Exports—$6.713 billion: garments, jute and jute goods, leather, frozen fish and seafood

Currency exchange rate: U.S. $1 = 59.65 Bangladesh takas (December 2004)

*GDP, or gross domestic product, is the total value of goods and services produced in a country annually (here estimated using the purchasing power parity method).

All figures are 2004 estimates unless otherwise noted.

Sources: CIA World Factbook, 2004; Bloomberg.com.

machinery and techniques have found their way to Bangladesh, on many of these small farms, oxen still pull the plows used to till the soil. This lack of mechanization is one reason that Bangladesh must import food to feed its population, despite the high proportion of the workforce in the agricultural sector.

Bangladesh ranks as one of the world's leading rice-growing countries.

Rice grows in almost all areas of the country, and if climate conditions are favorable, farmers can harvest three crops in a year.

Wheat is another major crop. Bangladesh also produces tea, sugarcane, potatoes, oilseeds, spices, fruit, tobacco, and legumes such as peas, lentils, and beans. Tea is grown on hillsides in the Chittagong Hill Tracts and the Sylhet District in northeastern Bangladesh.

Besides cultivating crops, many farmers raise livestock. Although the cattle are like the people they serve—often underfed and undernourished—they provide a valuable commodity. Bangladesh is a leading supplier of animal hides and skins for the world market.

Bangladesh is the world's leading producer of jute, which is used to make products such as twine, burlap bags, and carpet backing. While jute remains an important export, international demand has decreased somewhat because of the development of synthetic fibers.

Industry

Bangladesh's industrial sector accounts for more than one-quarter of GDP, though it employs only about 1 in 10 workers. Bangladesh has a thriving textile industry, with modern factories producing garments for overseas markets. In fact, clothing is the country's leading manufactured product, accounting for more than half of Bangladesh's 2004 export income of about $6.7 billion. Other factories manufacture agricultural equipment, leather goods, matches, and newsprint. Sugar, tea, cement, and chemical fertilizers are also processed in Bangladesh.

Fishing and fish processing is another major industry. Bangladesh is a nation of rivers, and its waterways provide an abundant source of fish. Bangladeshis catch large quantities of fish for their own consumption; frozen fish and seafood are also exported.

Craft production is an important business in Bangladesh's domestic economy. In rural areas Hindu craftspeople—weavers, potters, iron and

A Bangladeshi girl carries a load of jute. Long an important agricultural product of Bangladesh, jute is used to make twine, burlap, and carpet backing.

gold smiths, and carpenters—make traditional and practical items. These craftspeople and local farmers sell their goods and agricultural produce at village bazaars. Ten or so villages are linked in a market system centered on the weekly bazaar. The farmers are not only merchants, but also consumers purchasing spices, kerosene, soap, vegetables or fish, and salt from other merchants.

Services, Communications, and Infrastructure

In 2004 Bangladesh's service sector contributed an estimated 51.7 percent of GDP, but it employed only half that proportion of the labor force (26 percent). Prominent segments of the service sector include transportation, government administration, and banking and finance.

Bangladeshis usually find transportation by some kind of boat. They move about along 4,500 miles (7,200 km) of navigable waterways in small wooden boats and canoes. The major rivers carry passenger and cargo ships between the largest cities and towns. Chittagong, near the Bay of Bengal, is the major seaport. Major river ports include Dhaka, Narayanganj, Barisal, Khulna, and Chandpur.

Because Bangladesh is prone to heavy flooding and is crisscrossed by waterways, building roads throughout the country and bridges across the many rivers and streams is not practical. Recent estimates by the CIA World Factbook indicate that Bangladesh has slightly more than 12,000 miles (about 20,000 kilometers) of paved roads, along with approximately 1,700 miles (2,700 km) of railroad track. In Dhaka and other major cities, people are transported around in highly decorated taxis and rickshaws, three-wheeled vehicles with one passenger seat. Many of the rickshaws are motor driven, some are pedaled like a bicycle, and a few are actually pulled by a man on foot.

Bangladesh is a leading manufacturer of clothing, and much of it is exported to the United States and Europe.

Major airline services are available at Zia International Airport in Dhaka. Biman Bangladesh Airlines connects the capital city with more than two dozen major cities in the world, including London, Hong Kong, Tokyo, and Athens. Domestic flights take passengers to airports in Chittagong, Sylhet, Jessore, Cox's Bazar, Rajshahi, and Saidpur.

The government owns and operates Bangladesh's only television station, as well as nine radio stations. Comparatively few Bangladeshi families own TV sets or radios, particularly in the rural areas; villagers often gather in cafés or other public places to listen to radio broadcasts. Telephone services, also operated by the government, must be modernized if Bangladesh hopes to create a competitive economy. Few rural homes have telephone lines, though more than 1.3 million cell phones were in use in Bangladesh by 2003.

Bangladesh has a central bank, the Bangladesh Bank, which was established as soon as the country gained independence. Formerly the eastern wing of the State Bank of Pakistan, the Bangladesh Bank handles such functions as issuing currency, keeping reserve deposits, formulating and managing all monetary policies, and regulating traditional and non-traditional credit methods.

A Revolution in Loans

When economics professor Muhammad Yunus established the Grameen Bank in 1983, his goal was to grant loans to the poorest Bangladeshis. *Grameen* means "rural" in Bangla, and the project began in the tiny village of Jobra in the Chittagong District. Yunus had observed that women in Jobra who earned their meager livelihood making stools were trapped in a cycle of poverty. Because they had no money to buy bamboo—the raw material for the stools—they had to borrow from local moneylenders, who charged high interest. And since the finished stools fetched a low price, there was barely anything left over after the moneylenders were

With micro-credit loans from the Grameen Bank, founded by Muhammad Yunus (inset), these Bangladeshi "phone ladies" are purchasing cellular phones. They will take the phones to their home villages and make them available to customers who pay by the call. This small business works because much of rural Bangladesh remains without phone service, or even electricity.

repaid, so the women were forced to borrow again. Yunus contributed $27 of his own money to 42 stool makers in Jobra, and this became the first Grameen micro-credit loan. Yunus's small, informal loan helped lift these 42 women from the bonds of destitution—and started an economic revolution. Today, the Grameen Bank has advanced more than $3 billion in small loans of between $100 and $500 to over 2 million Bangladeshi families.

Yunus's belief that credit is a fundamental human right that should be extended to poor people has been embraced in nearly 100 countries. More than 250 institutions worldwide operate micro-credit programs that make small loans, then teach borrowers sound financial principles to help them succeed in their cottage industry or small business endeavor.

Politics and Government

In the 35-odd years of its existence as an independent state, Bangladesh has experienced much political upheaval. The country's constitution, which went into effect on December 16, 1972, established a democratic, parliamentary system of government. Yet assassinations, coups, and declarations of martial law—to say nothing of mass demonstrations and general strikes—have plagued the young country's political culture.

Bangladesh was just four years old when the first major political upheaval occurred. Sheikh Mujibur Rahman, who had defied the Pakistani government and was imprisoned for treason, was assassinated by some of the army officers who had helped win Bangladesh's independence in 1971.

The People's Republic of Bangladesh, as it is formally known, is divided into six administrative divisions: Barisal, Chittagong, Dhaka, Khulna, Rajshahi, and Sylhet. These divisions, named after their respective capitals, are subdivided into 64 districts, or *zillas*, the largest units of local government.

At the national level, the government is divided into the executive, legislative, and judicial branches. All citizens 18 years of age and older may vote in national elections for the parliamentary representatives from their district.

The executive branch is made up of the prime minister, the president, and a cabinet of ministers. The duties of the president, who is elected by the National Parliament for a five-year term, are mostly ceremonial but take on critical importance during the times when Parliament is dissolved. At those times the president is empowered, by the 13th amendment to Bangladesh's constitution (known as the Caretaker Government

Amendment), to direct the government and supervise the setting up of new parliamentary elections. On September 6, 2002, Iajuddin Ahmed, the only candidate to run, was sworn in as president for a five-year term.

The head of government is the prime minister. Officially appointed by the president, the prime minister is the leader of the political party that wins the most seats in Parliament in national elections. With the president's approval, the prime minister selects cabinet members to head the departments that manage government operations.

The elections of October 10, 2001, swept Khaleda Zia into the prime minister's office. Zia—the widow of Ziaur Rahman, founder of the Bangladesh Nationalist Party—forged a coalition between the BNP and other political parties, including Jamaat-e-Islami, Islami Oikya Jote, and the Jatiya Party, and defeated the powerful Awami League. Her term in office was set to run until 2006.

Bangladesh's legislative branch consists of the unicameral (single-chamber) Jatiya Sangsad, or National Parliament. Its 300 members, elected by popular vote from single territorial districts, serve five-year terms. As of early 2005, the BNP held 191 seats, while its main rival, the Awami League, had 62 seats.

Bangladesh's legal system is based on English common law—a legacy of British colonial rule on the Indian subcontinent. At the head of the judicial branch is the Supreme Court. It is divided into the Appellate Division, which hears appeals, and the High Court Division, which supervises all the lower courts. Justices and judges are appointed by the president. Local disputes are taken to district courts in the district capitals. Two common complaints about the court system are the backlog of cases and the prevalence of corruption. In a recent survey, more than 60 percent of the families involved in court cases reported having had to bribe court officials to obtain justice.

Police forces cover the towns and cities, but not the rural areas. If a serious crime or conflict occurs in a rural area, it may take days for the

Supporters of the opposition Awami League protest government policies at a December 2004 demonstration in Dhaka. Almost since independence, Bangladesh's political culture has been rent by bitter divisions, with general strikes, national protests, and an occasional coup impeding development.

police to arrive. Without police and nearby courts of law, rural communities rely on an informal system of social control. For instance, a crowd might gather to beat an apprehended thief. When serious disputes arise between families, the heads of families or community leaders step in to negotiate. Once a decision is made, the offending party must pay restitution in money or in land. Village councils, made up of the most respected members of the community, often settle nonviolent disagreements. Sometimes the police are called in, but they are often paid off to ensure that they let the local people handle the issue independently.

Bangladesh's military was established in 1971 as the Mukti Bahini, the guerrilla resistance army that fought West Pakistan. After independence, many of these freedom fighters became part of the regular army, navy, or air force. Bangladesh also supports a militia at the local level.

Twice since independence, the military has seized control of the government. The military has also been called on to put down one rebellion, waged by the Shanti Bahini insurgents in the Chittagong Hill Tracts. The insurgents were Jummas, as the Chittagong Hill Tract tribal groups are collectively called, who opposed the migration of settlers into their region. These settlers were usually Muslims who brought their customs and culture into an area where the tribal groups were mostly Buddhist and Hindu. Fighting broke out in early 1976 and finally ended more than 20 years later, in 1997, when the Jummas and the government reached a peace

The disk near the center of Bangladesh's flag—the "red sun of freedom"—symbolizes the blood that was shed for independence. The green field represents Bangladesh's lush countryside; green is also the traditional color of Islam, the state religion.

agreement. However, the situation remains tense, with Jummas complaining that the government has not honored the conditions of the peace accord; the Zia administration, for its part, has stated that it has already made too many concessions to the tribal groups.

Religion

Religion is a powerful force in Bangladesh, and Islam is by far the most widely practiced faith. More than 8 in 10 Bangladeshis follow Islam, with the vast majority belonging to the orthodox Sunni branch. In 1988 Bangladesh's constitution was amended to establish Islam as the state religion, though citizens are free to practice whatever faith they choose.

Like their co-religionists throughout the world, Bangladesh's Muslims believe that the prophet Muhammad, an Arab merchant born in Mecca (in present-day Saudi Arabia) around A.D. 570, received a series of revelations from Allah, or God, beginning in 610. These revelations were later transcribed in the Qur'an (or Koran), Islam's holy book.

Islam is a monotheistic faith that has a fair amount in common with Judaism and Christianity, including central figures such as Noah (Nuh), Moses (Musa), Abraham (Ibrahim), and Jesus (Isa)—all of whom are considered prophets in the Islamic tradition. Muslims believe that Muhammad was God's last and greatest prophet.

The basic obligations of Muslims are encapsulated in the so-called Five Pillars of Islam: 1) the *Shahada,* or profession of faith ("There is no God but Allah, and Muhammad is His messenger"); 2) prayers performed five times daily while facing in the direction of Mecca; 3) almsgiving or charity toward the poor; 4) fasting between dawn and dusk during the holy month of Ramadan; and 5) the hajj, or pilgrimage to Mecca, which every Muslim tries to make at least once in his or her lifetime.

In Bangladesh, as in many Muslim societies, men enjoy considerably more authority and freedom than women, who must avoid social contact

Bangladesh's more conservative Muslims (along with some Hindus) practice purdah, which dictates that women must be covered up when in public—if they leave the house at all.

with males who are not family members. Bangladesh's more conservative Muslims (along with some Hindus) practice *purdah*, a tradition that is also prevalent in India and Pakistan and has as much basis in culture as in religion. Purdah is the seclusion of women from public view, and it requires that women who are outside their home be veiled; many Bangladeshi women who follow the tradition rarely leave their house at all, and when visitors come, they stay in their own room or in the kitchen.

About 16 percent of Bangladesh's population is Hindu. Unlike Muslims, Hindus worship multiple gods and goddesses, including Krishna, Ram, Durga, Kali, and Ganesh. Many Bangladeshi Hindus celebrate rituals dedicated to the female goddess Durga. Brahman priests perform rituals for the Hindu community; in general these are not as rigidly structured as are Islamic rituals.

The caste system divides Hindus into different social classes that observe their own customs and rules of behavior. The caste system limits social interactions with members of other castes. Hindu parents arrange marriages for their children, and intermarriage between castes is rare. Although Hindu women have few legal rights, they do have more social freedom than Muslim women.

Religions other than Islam and Hinduism account for only about 1 percent of the population of Bangladesh. These include Buddhism and Christianity.

With more than 141 million people living in an area about the size of Wisconsin, Bangladesh is the most densely populated country in the world that is not an island. Shown here is a street scene from Dhaka.

5

The People

With an estimated 2004 population of more than 141 million, Bangladesh is the world's eighth most populous country. Yet it ranks as the 92nd largest country by total area—which means that Bangladesh is among the most densely populated countries in the world. An average of more than 2,540 Bangladeshis crowd together per square mile (981 people per square kilometer); by comparison, population density in the United States is more than 30 times lower, about 83 people per square mile (32 per sq km). Crowded conditions in Bangladesh help contribute to disease, extreme poverty, and a poor quality of living.

Ethnically, Bangladesh is a homogeneous country: 98 percent of its citizens are Bengali. Not surprisingly, the Bengalis' native tongue, Bangla (also known as Bengali), is the country's official language. Most

The People of Bangladesh

Population: 141,340,476
Ethnic groups: Bengali, 98%; tribal groups, non-Bengali
    Muslims, 2% (1998 est.)
Religions: Muslim, 83%; Hindu, 16%; other, 1% (1998)
Age structure:
    0–14 years: 33.5%
    15–64 years: 63.1%
    65 years and over: 3.4%
Population growth rate: 2.08%
Birth rate: 30.03 births/1,000 population
Infant mortality rate: 64.32 deaths/1,000 live births
Death rate: 8.52 deaths/1,000 population
Life expectancy at birth:
    total population: 61.71 years
    male: 61.8 years
    female: 61.61 years
Total fertility rate: 3.15 children born/woman
Literacy: 43.1% (2003 est.)

All figures are 2004 estimates unless otherwise indicated.
Source: Adapted from CIA World Factbook, 2004.

Bangladeshis also speak the British form of English, a legacy of the British Raj.

Among the 2 percent of Bangladeshis who do not belong to the Bengali majority are 13 minority groups living in the Chittagong Hill Tracts of southeastern Bangladesh. Collectively they call themselves the Jumma people, and the largest of these groups are the Chakmas, the Marmas, the Mros, and the Tipperas. The Jummas differ from the Bengalis in race, religion, ethnicity, language, and culture. From 1976 until late 1997, major grievances and disputes arose between the Jummas and the Bangladeshi Muslims who moved into the area, and some of the Jummas fought a guerrilla campaign against the national government. A treaty ending the fighting was signed in December 1997.

Marriage, Family, and Gender Roles

Bangladesh is a **patriarchal** society, with men holding a disproportionate amount of power in all areas of life. Education is considered less necessary for women, and authority comes from a woman's father, older brother, or husband. Notwithstanding these constraints, some women attend universities and hold important positions in government and business. For example, two distinguished Muslim women, Begum Khaleda Zia and Sheikh Hasina Wazed, have risen to political power as prime ministers of the country, elected by a wide majority. In general, urban Muslim women have more mobility and freedom than do their counterparts living in rural areas.

Most women's responsibilities are restricted to running their households, raising children, and managing some family matters. Muslim women who practice purdah cannot travel in public places without being accompanied by a male family member. Even those who do not strictly follow purdah are not encouraged to go out in public or travel further than the homes of their immediate neighbors, unless accompanied by a male relative. Women are not allowed in the mosques, which are reserved for Muslim men only.

Men serve as head of the household and are expected to support their families. In rural areas, they handle most agricultural tasks. They also do most of the shopping, since women are prohibited or discouraged from the interaction of a crowded market. When not working, men often spend time drinking tea in cafés and socializing with other men outside their home.

In Bangladesh, arranged marriages are still the rule, and it is the father's prerogative to decide when his daughter should be wed. Women typically marry between the ages of 15 and 20; men are usually 5 to 10 years older than their wives.

How does a father find a husband for his daughter? He contacts agencies, go-betweens, relatives, and even friends to find an appropriate mate. Matches are based on factors such as the family's economic status, educational background, and religious devotion. Sometimes a father gives his daughter the important information about five or six potential husbands and lets her make the final decision. A marriage arrangement between two families may be sealed with a dowry and other gifts to the groom, particularly among less-educated families.

Divorce is rare because it carries a heavy social stigma. In keeping with Islamic custom, however, the decision on whether to divorce is solely in the hands of the husband, who must merely say "I divorce you" three times to dissolve the marriage. A divorced woman must return to her parents' household, where she is often not welcome.

Bangladeshis often live as extended families in what are known as *baris*. This family unit is made up of the husband and wife, their unmarried children, and their adult sons with their wives and children. Grandparents may be part of this extended family as well, and sometimes the husband's brothers, cousins, nieces, and nephews also live in the *bari*. In rural areas, the *bari* is often laid out with three or four houses facing each other in a square courtyard, where family members share food and carry out common tasks.

Authority in the *bari* rests with the oldest man, but the oldest woman also wields considerable power within the household. Young couples are expected to contribute their earnings to the head of the household. Children in the extended family are at the bottom of the hierarchy. Child care is the responsibility of older sisters as well as their mother.

Education

In Bangladesh education is free and begins at age five or six for boys and girls. Primary school runs from grades 1 through 5; secondary runs from grades 6 through 10. Higher secondary, grades 11 and 12, is open to students who qualify on the secondary school certificate examination. At the end of grade 12, students take another examination; if they score high enough, they can qualify for entrance into one of the universities.

Approximately 75 percent of Bangladesh's children go to primary school, which is supposed to be required for those aged 6 through 11. However, the law is not enforced, so many—especially the very poor—do not finish their primary education. As children get older and become more productive members of their households, they tend to attend school less. In rural areas these children may haul water, watch animals, and help with processing the harvested crop. In urban areas, children may drop out of school to take factory jobs or perform low-paying work such as shining shoes and painting rickshaws. Girls who drop out typically manage household chores and care for younger siblings.

In conservative, patriarchal Bangladesh, education is considered more important for boys than for girls. Over half of all males age 15 and older can read and write, compared with just 3 in 10 females. Here boys read from their books in a public school in Dhaka.

A greater number of boys than girls complete their primary education. Also, the higher a family's socioeconomic status, the more likely its children will finish primary school. Only about 17 percent of Bangladeshi students receive their secondary education and continue on to a college or university. University students usually come from well-off families, who can afford the costs.

Competition to qualify for university admission is intense. High status and good job opportunities await those who have university degrees. Higher education follows the British model, except that a degree may require more than the usual four years to complete. Bangladesh has a number of large universities offering undergraduate through postgraduate degrees. Dhaka University, established in 1921, is the oldest institution of comprehensive higher education in Bangladesh. Rajshahi University opened in 1954; Chittagong University admitted its first students in 1965; and Jahangirnagar University began accepting students in January 1971. Bangladesh also has a number of smaller public universities, private universities, and medical colleges, some of which are attached to the large public universities.

Most university students in Bangladesh join the student wing of a political party. Because students as well as faculty members tend to be politically active, they are often at the forefront of protests, strikes, and even violent demonstrations. Bangladesh's universities have frequently shut down during periods of political turmoil, and as a result it is not uncommon for students to take five to eight years to complete an undergraduate degree.

Education is frequently the key to finding employment outside the agricultural sector of the economy. Unfortunately, educated young men often find their employment chances extremely limited if they continue to live in their villages.

Housing and Daily Life

In Bangladesh's villages, people live in simple, functional rectangular structures constructed of dried mud, bamboo, or red brick with thatched roofs. For protection against flooding, many houses are built on top of earthen or wooden platforms. Houses typically have little decoration inside; wall space is used for storage. Few village homes have electricity. Furniture is minimal and may include a chair or table, a few low stools, and thin bamboo mats that serve as beds.

Many houses have verandas or roofed porches, and much of daily life takes place on these porches. The kitchen is a detached, smaller mud or bamboo structure. During the dry season, women often cook outdoors on hearths they construct in the household courtyard. Some families share their kitchen with other families.

In rural areas few homes have plumbing, and rivers and ponds are used for bathing as well as toilet functions. This makes the water dangerous to drink. Many diseases that afflict Bangladeshis are the result of unsafe water.

But sanitation is not just a rural problem. Many city dwellers are crowded together in small wooden houses, and in the poorest slums homes are made of cardboard, scraps of wood, or even sticks.

One of the missions of the Grameen Bank is to improve the quality of life for its clients, and sanitation is a major concern. The bank requires borrowers to create sanitation facilities and to drink only water from tube wells or water that has been boiled or chemically treated.

City dwellings demonstrate wealth and social rank just as homes in other parts of the world do. A concrete-faced house and a ceramic tile roof indicate that a wealthy family lives inside. Another sign of wealth is an individual's mode of transportation. Very few Bangladeshis—even those who are comparatively wealthy—can afford an automobile, but

Plumbing is absent in most of rural Bangladesh, forcing people to use rivers and ponds for bathing and toilet functions. This, in turn, compromises the safety of drinking water.

the well-off can purchase a motorcycle. Other indicators of wealth are telephones, color televisions, and electricity.

Differences in age and social standing are evident in the way Bangladeshis speak to one another. Individuals with higher status are not addressed by their personal names; instead, a title or kinship term is used.

Sports

Sports are quite popular in Bangladesh. The Bangladesh Sports Control Board lists 29 sports federations under its direction. These include federations for soccer (which is called football in Bangladesh); cricket, the well-known English ball and bat team game; field hockey; tennis; badminton; volleyball; and handball.

The national sport is *kabadi*, a game played by two 12-member teams. It is similar to the American children's game Red Rover in that a team forms a line and tries to keep players from the opposing team from breaking through their line. In many rural areas, *kabadi* is called *ha-du-du* and is less organized and rule-driven. In 1990 *kabadi* was part of the Asian Games held in Beijing, and Bangladesh brought home the silver medal in the event.

Board games are also popular pastimes. Chess is an important event for both men and women. Bangladeshi chess players participate in national and international tournaments. Another important board game is carom, a kind of billiards that is played by two to four persons. Carom tournaments take place at schools, colleges, universities, clubs, and societies throughout Bangladesh and other parts of Asia.

Clothing

Many Bangladeshis, particularly in cities, wear Western-style attire. Men of high standing may sport the traditional loose white cotton pants worn with a long white shirt. Wearing white shows

Soccer has long been among the most popular sports in Bangladesh, but it wasn't until October 2004 that the first women's tournament was held. Shown here is action from that groundbreaking competition.

that a man's occupation does not require any physical labor that would get his clothes dirty. A man of high social rank will not be seen carrying anything, but will instead assign that task to a laborer or an assistant. The majority of Bangladeshi males wear an ankle-length, skirt-like cloth garment called a *lungi*. Hindu men often wear a *dhoti*, a cloth wound around the waist and thighs. Clothing styles are loose and cool, important features in the hot, humid climate of Bangladesh.

For Bangladeshi women who do not wear Western-style clothing, the most common attire is the traditional sari, a long length of cloth wrapped around the waist and then draped over the shoulders and head. The sari is worn over a short blouse. Saris and the gold jewelry decorating them indicate social status. Women of high rank have elaborate and finely worked cloth. In fact, some of the finest saris in the world are made and worn in Bangladesh, which has a long, distinguished history of weaving. Poorer women wear cheap green or indigo saris made of rough, thick cotton.

Traditional Handicrafts

Hindus produce a large proportion of Bangladesh's traditional crafts. In the Hindu caste system, weavers, potters, and iron and gold smiths belong to the same caste as farmers, merchants, and traders. Many of the items they produce are used for everyday life. Pottery objects such as water jugs and bowls of red clay are not only useful household items, but they are frequently also works of art. Brightly painted clay sculptures depicting Ganesh, Durga, and other Hindu gods are also popular craft items.

One distinctive Bangladeshi art form can be seen in the vibrant paintings that decorate the backs of rickshaws, the wooden sides of trucks, and the backs of taxis. These paintings feature images of rural scenes, famous political figures, favorite film stars, famous events, and symbols.

The East Bengal region has long been known for its textiles. Although the renowned weavers of Dhaka have largely been replaced by the ready-made

Rickshaws are a major mode of transportation in Bangladesh's cities, and the vibrant paintings that adorn the backs of these vehicles constitute a popular art form.

clothing industry, a few still produce some of the world's finest fabrics. Rich brocades, silk and cotton saris, and stoles embroidered with silver and golden thread are available in specialty shops, markets, and bazaars. Some of these garments are made from the famous Dhaka ***muslin*** once worn by royal families.

Folklore, Food, and Entertainments

Folklore is part of the oral tradition of India and Bengal. Bengali culture includes fairy tales, some of which resemble the European tales of a prince's adventure to win the hand of a beautiful princess. However, unlike Western fairy tales, Bengali stories do not have fairies. Hero stories, tall tales, and riddles also are part of the folklore passed from generation to generation.

Dance in Bangladesh stems from folklore and rural culture. Bengali dance is mostly a female-only endeavor using hand, feet, and head movements. Many dances are based on classical Indian forms; others, like the Manipuri, stem from the customs and beliefs of individual tribes. Originally, tribal dances had no elaborate staging or musical arrange-

Most traditional Bengali dance forms are reserved for women. These dancers are performing at the festival of Basanta, which welcomes the arrival of spring.

ments: the dancers sang while they performed. Television and tourism have helped modernize the art form, and today dancers perform on stage with lighting, makeup, and musical instruments.

Folk theater, a mixture of poetry, dance, and drama based on religious stories, is another popular form of entertainment. Traveling shows perform plays throughout the countryside. In urban areas, the universities sometimes sponsor productions.

Rice and fish form the foundation of the Bangladeshi diet. Lamb is a popular meat because eating it does not violate any dietary restrictions of Islam or Hinduism (Muslims do not consume pork, and Hindus do not eat beef). Many Bengali dishes are cooked in spicy curry (*torkari*) sauces, which consist of a blend of several spices ranging from mild to very hot. Another favorite dish is kabobs made with chunks of fish, vegetables, poultry, or lamb skewered together and grilled. Kabobs and most other foods are served with rice. One food that is increasingly popular is *ruti*, a wheat-based flat bread that is served with curries at the evening meal and at breakfast. Bangladeshis also favor *dal*, a thin soup made of ground lentils, chickpeas, or other legumes that is poured over rice. Dessert is often *misti dohi*, a sweetened yogurt; *zorda*, sweetened rice with nuts; or *firni*, a kind of rice pudding. Bangladeshis also enjoy a variety of cakes and pastries that are collectively called *pitha*.

Breakfast is the most varied of the meals: sometimes it is rice-based; sometimes it is bread-based. One favorite breakfast called *pantabhat* consists of leftover cold rice in water or milk mixed with *gur* (date palm sugar).

Water and tea are the most commonly served beverages. Many men in the cities like to drink a cup of sweet tea with milk (*cha*) at a small tea stall. *Lassi,* another popular drink, is made from yogurt. Bangladeshis like to snack on small fried items, fruit, and puffed rice.

In the rural areas, a nearby river supplies fish. Fruit trees such as mango and jackfruit grow around or close to homesteads. Jackfruit, the

A Bangladeshi woman displays a plate of *nakshi pitha*, a sweet cake that is a favorite treat in rural areas.

world's largest tree-borne fruit, sometimes grows to a weight of 100 pounds (45 kilograms). The ripe yellow-orange flesh tastes like a mix of pineapple, banana, and mango and is a staple of the Bangladeshi diet.

A special ritual precedes every meal in Bangladesh. The right hand is washed with water above the eating bowl. Then, using the right hand, each person rubs the interior of the bowl, discards the water, and fills the bowl with food. When the meal is finished, each person washes his or her right hand again, holding it over the empty bowl. The left hand is never used to consume food.

Food plays a major role in many holidays and celebrations. At weddings, *biryani*, a rice dish with lamb or beef and a blend of spices, is often served. For these special occasions the rice is a finer, thinner-grained type. If *biryani* is not offered, a multicourse meal is provided, one course at a time. This meal includes chicken, fish, vegetable, goat, or beef curries, along with *dal*. The meal is finished with a bit of rice and sweet yogurt.

Music and Literature

The Bangla Academy in Dhaka supports many of Bangladesh's writers, poets, and musicians. Rabindranath Tagore (1861–1941), a champion of the Bengali language and culture, won the 1913 Nobel Prize in literature; he was the first Asian writer to achieve this distinction. Tagore is one of the country's most revered heroes; the lyrics to Bangladesh's national anthem are taken from his poem "Golden Bengal."

The poetry of Kazi Nazrul Islam (1899–1976), the national poet of Bangladesh, expresses a fierce resistance to all forms of repression. Islam was also a composer who established his own genre by modernizing traditional Bengali songs. Taslima Nasreen is among the most famous of contemporary Bangladeshi writers. Her novels and essays question the Islamic treatment of women. Because she has riled many conservative Muslims, she lives in exile, but she continues to write about the plight of Muslim women.

Tagore, Nazrul, and other poets have had significant influence on their country's music. They breathed new life into the traditional melodic patterns called *ragas* and introduced new rhythms (known as *talas*) into Bangla songs. Bangladesh has a rich folk music tradition that includes religious and secular (non-religious) songs. Folk songs deal with themes such as festivals, the natural beauty of the country, and life on the rivers. The most commonly used instruments in Bangladesh's music are the sitar, tabla, and harmonium. Singers may be accompanied by the *ektara*, a one-stringed instrument made from the shell of a bottle gourd, wood apple, or coconut or sometimes constructed of wood or brass.

Celebrations and Festivals

Bangladeshis of all ages and religious persuasions observe three national days. February 21, National Martyr's Day, commemorates the lives lost during the Language Movement of 1952; Independence Day is celebrated on March 26; and December 16, Victory Day, marks the end of the nine-month struggle against Pakistan. These events are celebrated with parades and political speeches. The Bengali New Year celebration, held on April 13 or 14, includes poetry readings and musical events. May Day (May 1) recognizes the efforts of workers with speeches and cultural events.

Bangladeshis celebrate several religious holidays as well. Hindus observe Saraswati Puja in February; this is an important occasion for stu-

Former prime minister Sheikh Hasina Wazed and other leaders of the Awami League commemorate Victory Day (December 16) by placing a wreath at a memorial to the fallen in Dhaka.

dents, since Saraswati is the patron of learning. Durga Puja is a nine-day festival in October honoring the warrior goddess Durga. In November the female deity Kali is honored with Kali Puja, a festival of lights. Candles are lit in and around Hindu homes for this celebration.

For Muslims, Ramadan, the ninth month of the Islamic lunar year, is a particularly important time. During Ramadan the faithful fast from dawn to dusk, eating and drinking only before the sun rises and after it sets. Eid al-Fitr (the Feast of Fast-Breaking), which marks the end of the holy month, is a three-day event that many Bangladeshis turn into a weeklong celebration. On Eid al-Fitr, Bangladeshis dress up, prepare special foods, and even exchange Eid cards. Muslims also give money to those less fortunate, beginning with relatives, then neighbors, and finally to the poor in general. During Eid, city dwellers often return to their native villages. Family identity is important, and even though family members may no longer live in the countryside, they still make it a point to take this annual trip to their ancestral home. In the villages, Eid fairs are organized on the bank of a river or under a big banyan tree near the local bazaar. Handicraft items are sold, along with musical instruments and a variety of foods and sweets. Larger fairs offer merry-go-rounds and puppet shows as well as folk music and dancing. In some of the river communities, boat races are a major attraction, as are sports competitions.

Eid al-Adha (the Feast of the Sacrifice) is another important Islamic holiday. It falls on the 10th day of the last month on the Islamic lunar calendar. Muslims with sufficient means mark the occasion by slaughtering a goat or cow and giving a portion of the meat to relatives and to the poor. The fresh meat is typically used to make curries.

In teeming Dhaka, slums sprawl in the shadow of modern high-rises that attest to the city's vitality as a center of commerce, education, culture, and government.

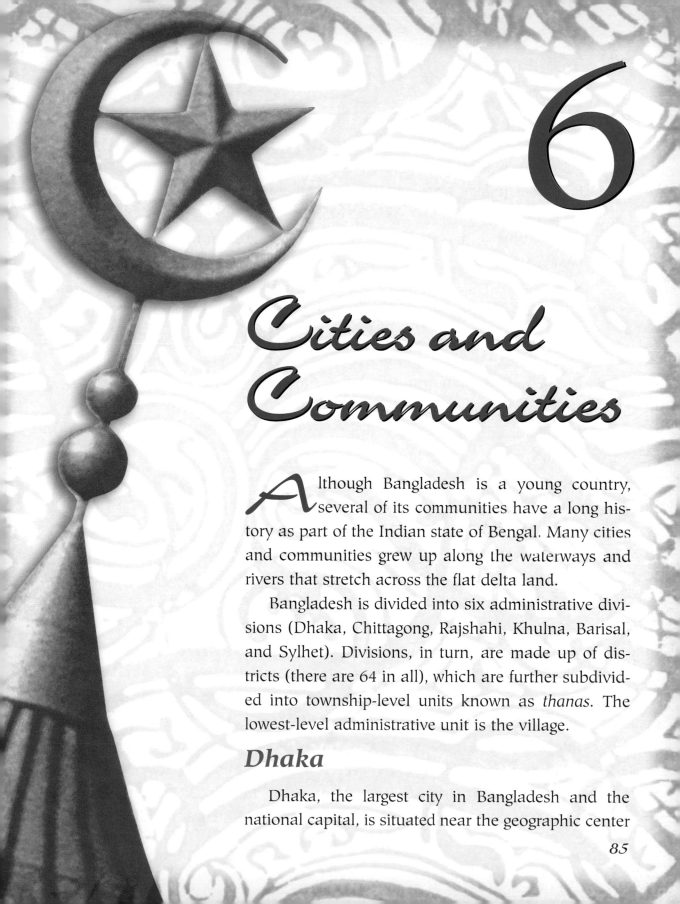

6

Cities and Communities

A lthough Bangladesh is a young country, several of its communities have a long history as part of the Indian state of Bengal. Many cities and communities grew up along the waterways and rivers that stretch across the flat delta land.

Bangladesh is divided into six administrative divisions (Dhaka, Chittagong, Rajshahi, Khulna, Barisal, and Sylhet). Divisions, in turn, are made up of districts (there are 64 in all), which are further subdivided into township-level units known as *thanas*. The lowest-level administrative unit is the village.

Dhaka

Dhaka, the largest city in Bangladesh and the national capital, is situated near the geographic center of the country in the delta region of the Ganges and Brahmaputra Rivers. The city sits on the bank of the Buriganga River. Including its surrounding suburbs, Dhaka covers an area of some 315 square miles (815 sq km) and had an estimated 2004 population numbering more than 10 million.

Dhaka's history goes back more than a millennium. Tribes from South Asia settled on the site in the seventh century A.D. For many years, Hindu kings ruled Dhaka; they were followed by the Pala and Sena dynasties (ca. 750–1000). In the 15th century the city was an established center of government under the Delhi Sultanate as Muslim rulers gained control of the delta area. In 1608 Dhaka became the capital of Bengal, by that point a territory of the Mughal Empire. A century and a half later, in 1765, Dhaka came under British control and lost some of its political importance. However, the city's commercial enterprises continued to thrive, and the cotton textile industry (particularly muslin) made Dhaka famous.

As the capital of East Pakistan, Dhaka (then spelled *Dacca*) was the center of Bengali disaffection with the Pakistani national government. The worst violence growing out of the Language Movement, for example, took place in Dhaka. In 1982 the spelling of the city was changed to its current Bengali form as a testament to the Bengali heritage.

Today the Shahid Minar (Martyrs' Monument) in Dhaka is a symbol of Bengali nationalism, commemorating those who gave their lives for the preservation of the Bengali language. On February 21, people honor those slain by thronging the monument and covering it with wreaths and flowers.

Almost 93 percent of Dhaka's residents are Muslim, and the domes, minarets, and pointed arches of the city's more than 700 mosques are an integral part of its character. These mosques are found throughout Dhaka's two major sections: the old city and the new city. The old city includes the waterfront, main shopping district, and a bustling outdoor market known as the Chauk. Yachts, motor launches, paddle-steamers, and fishermen's boats crowd the Sadarghat waterfront on the bank of the Buriganga River. Sadarghat is also home to crowded slums.

One of the newest and fastest-growing sections of Dhaka is Ramna, on the northern edge of the city. Many middle-class and wealthy citizens live in this area, which features tree-lined streets, parks, and a shopping district. The University of Dhaka, one of Bangladesh's finest universities, is located in Ramna as well.

Dhaka boasts many attractions, including the Bangladesh National Museum, National Art Gallery, Mirpur Zoo, and Botanical Garden. Some of the most visible attractions are the brightly decorated rickshaws and baby taxis that transport Bangladeshis and tourists around the city. Rickshaws are a major source of income throughout Bangladesh, but particularly in Dhaka. Hundreds of thousands of people in the city earn their livelihoods from the rickshaw business—as pullers and drivers, vehicle manufacturers, or artists who decorate the bodies of the rickshaws.

Baby taxis provide another source of income and transportation. These vehicles—modeled on the Vespa motor scooter, which is made in India—consist of three wheels, an engine, and a front seat protected by a windshield. The coach, made of wood covered with aluminum sheets, is topped with fabric stitched to fit the frame, and the interior seat is upholstered in the same fabric. The bodies of baby taxis are painted black, but the backs are adorned with colorful paintings, many of which are executed with considerable skill. Like rickshaws, baby taxis create jobs. Assembling one baby taxi takes about 12 hours, a typical workday for many Bangladeshis.

Because Dhaka is built on the river delta, the surrounding countryside of the Dhaka Division is fertile. It is, in fact, one of the world's leading rice- and jute-growing areas. Dhaka Division is also the nation's commercial and industrial center. Factories operate all over the city and in the outlying districts, producing cotton fabrics, glass, leather, metals, sugar, and jute products. Dhaka continues to produce some of the finest cotton fabrics, made in the small shops of local weavers and in large factories.

Chittagong Division

Chittagong, the capital of the Chittagong Division, is Bangladesh's second most populous urban area, with an estimated 2004 population of 3.3 million. Located on the Karnaphuli River about 12 miles (19 km) from where it empties into the Bay of Bengal, Chittagong is the country's chief seaport. Chittagong is also Bangladesh's commercial and manufacturing center; a nearby hydroelectric plant generates power for many of the city's industries.

Chittagong, located on the Karnaphuli River near the Bay of Bengal, is Bangladesh's chief seaport. It is a center of shipbuilding as well as ship dismantling. The workers in this photograph are carrying a piece of steel salvaged from a large oceangoing vessel.

Chittagong has a long history. Mentioned by a Chinese traveler in the seventh century A.D., it was an important link in the spice trade between the East and Europe. Today, the most lucrative resources of the area are jute, cotton, rice, tea, petroleum from offshore installations, and bamboo.

Chittagong has many interesting places to visit. These include the multi-domed Chandanpura Mosque, located in the old city. The Circuit House, formerly a government building, is an attractive structure with a bloody past. The most recent tragedy that occurred in the building was the assassination of President Ziaur Rahman on May 30, 1981. The Circuit House has since been converted into the Zia Museum in honor of the slain leader. Standing as a reminder of the former power of the British East India Company is the Court Building Museum; its hundreds of rooms cover some 250,000 square feet (more than 23,000 square meters). The Ethnological Museum houses collections of artifacts reflecting the tribal culture and heritage of Bangladesh.

The Chittagong Division is a picturesque region of coconut palms, rivers, and green hills, some of them rising to 4,000 feet (1,219 meters). The division shares its northern border with the tea-growing Indian state of Assam and shares its eastern border with Burma.

The cultural diversity of the region is evidenced by a variety of Buddhist, Hindu, Muslim, and European artifacts. The Buddhists built monasteries, and while many of the ancient structures have long since crumbled, some of these ruins have been collected and displayed by the Mainamati Archaeological Museum. Many mosques and other examples of Islamic architecture from the Mughal Empire are still standing in the Chittagong Division. And relics of the Portuguese (who arrived in the 16th century) and of the British (who controlled the area from the 18th to the 20th centuries) can also be seen.

One of the most vibrant parts of the Chittagong Division is the Chittagong Hill Tracts—5,093 square miles (13,191 sq km) of rugged, thick forests along the Bay of Bengal. The Chittagong Hill Tracts is divided into three districts: Rangamati, Khagrachari, and Bandarban. Most of the inhabitants of these districts are members of one of the 13 tribal peoples collectively known as the Jummas. The Jummas are very self-reliant: they grow their own food, weave their own clothes, and live simply.

Rangamati, the capital of the Chittagong Hill Tracts, sits on an isthmus projecting into Kaptai Lake. This man-made body of water was formed by the damming of the Karnaphuli River. With its scenic countryside and tribespeople selling beautiful homespun textile products and ivory jewelry, Rangamati is a popular tourist spot. Every year in mid-April, a widely attended Buddhist water festival takes place on Kaptai Lake.

The tourist capital of Bangladesh, Cox's Bazar, is part of the Chittagong Division. Miles of golden sand beaches, towering cliffs, rare conch shells, and Buddhist attractions have made this city one of the most visited places in Bangladesh. Inani Beach, which stretches for some 75 miles (120 km), has the distinction of being the longest beach in the world.

Cox's Bazar gets its name from Captain Hiram Cox, who in 1798 was commissioned to settle the area with immigrants fleeing from Burma. But the region had been occupied earlier by the Mogh people, Hindu and Buddhist ethnic groups who came from China and Burma. At one point, Cox's Bazar was populated with Mogh pirates who, during the 17th century, conspired with Portuguese thieves to plunder the Bay of Bengal. Though they no longer make their livelihood through piracy, the Mogh people still live in the region. They have preserved their tribal ways as well as their reputation as skilled craftsmen.

Khulna

Located on the Rupsa River in southwestern Bangladesh, Khulna is the capital of the Khulna Division. This important river port, gateway to the Sundarbans, is also Bangladesh's third-largest city, with more than 1.3

Women set out fish to dry at a fish-processing center in Cox's Bazar.

million residents in 2004. It is connected to the major southern delta cities by rail, roadway, and river steamer. Along with its successful shipbuilding industry, the city supports a match factory; a sawmill; and paper, hardboard, textile, steel, rice, and flour enterprises. Like Dhaka and Chittagong, Khulna has a university as well as a medical college.

Khulna Division is an important trade and produce collection center. It is also the hub of the country's shipbuilding industy, with shipyards located on the Kazibacha River. In addition, Khulna hosts a naval base as well as telephone cable and newsprint industries.

The Khulna Division contains the Sundarbans, home of the largest mangrove forest in the world. Fishing is an important industry in this area, which attracts fishermen from all over the country between mid-October

Shops line this street in Khulna, Bangladesh's third-largest city.

and mid-February. During these months, fishermen can be seen drying their catch on the sunny beaches of the island of Dublar Char. The Sundarbans forest is also a major source of honey and beeswax. Honey collectors journey to the forests during April and May. Others are drawn to the Sundarbans by the prospect of glimpsing the Royal Bengal tigers or the numerous other animal and plant species.

The human inhabitants of this region number only about 300,000. In addition to fishing, many make their livelihood as woodcutters. The only way to travel inside the swampy forests is by boat. Boats even serve as homes for many residents. If people decide to live on the land, they construct dwellings atop wooden poles to protect themselves from the wild animals at the edge of the forest.

Rajshahi

The Rajshahi Division of Bangladesh is famous for its silk production. In fact, the division capital of the same name, located on the Padma River in the northwest region, is known by the nickname the City of Silk.

> The Buddhist monastery of Somapuri Vihara—located at Paharpur, a village in the Rajshahi Division—dates from the eighth century A.D. Covering about 27 acres (11 hectares) of land, the monastery had room for more than 170 monks and is considered one of the most important ruins of ancient Buddhism south of the Himalayas. Recently, a museum was established on the site to house objects recovered from archaeological excavations.

Rajshahi is the fourth-largest city in Bangladesh; its estimated 2004 population stood at about 668,400.

The Rajshahi region has a rich history. It was once controlled by the ancient Vanga rulers. Much later, the region's prime location and its silk production attracted foreign settlers. During the 17th century, the region flourished as the Dutch, French, and British East India companies established business operations there.

In addition to its thriving silk industry, Rajshahi Division has an aluminum factory, iron mill, textile mill, flour and rice mill, and match factory. Other manufactured products include pharmaceuticals, *jarda* (scented tobacco), and plastics.

Sylhet

Sylhet town, located on the Surma River 120 miles (193 km) northeast of Dhaka, is a division capital whose 2004 population stood at about 295,000. Many historians believe that Sylhet (also known by its ancient name of Srihatta, meaning "enriched market place") was a commercial center of the ancient world. The town, as well as the valley it sits in, was long ruled by local chieftains. In 1303, however, the Muslim leader Hazrat Shah Jalal brought Islam to the area. According to legend, Jalal—whose courageous feats are commemorated by a famous shrine in Sylhet town—

This young woman is picking tea leaves on a plantation in the Sylhet Division.

defeated the Hindu raja and transformed the raja's followers into catfish, which still live in the tank adjacent to the shrine.

On June 12, 1897, an earthquake destroyed the town of Sylhet. From the wreckage, a town modeled after European cities was built.

The Sylhet Division is Bangladesh's tea-growing area, with beautiful plantations located alongside lush forests. The Bangladesh Tea Research Institute, where all stages of tea cultivation and processing are exhibited, is located in Sylhet.

In addition to the tea plantations, the Sylhet region's economy is bolstered by a fertilizer plant and a natural gas plant, along with various handicraft operations. Cane products include chairs, tables, tea trays, flower vases, and bags. *Shital pati*, a kind of handmade mat of cane, is another famous product of the region.

The Sylhet Division is home to some aboriginal tribes, such as the Tipperas, Manipuris, Khasis, and Garos. These tribes continue to practice their ancient rituals and customs. The Manipuri Dance, performed during the festival of Rash Leela, preserves an old tradition of pairing boys and girls.

Barisal

Barisal, capital of the division of the same name, is a growing city whose estimated 2004 population stood at about 254,000. Established in 1957, Barisal sits on the Kirtan Khola River, near the mouth of the Meghna, and is headquarters to the Bangladesh Inland Water Transport Authority. Among its many industries are pharmaceuticals, jute, rice, textiles, and flour. It is also home to seed-oil mills, a biscuit factory, and an ice factory.

In addition, Barisal has a thriving cottage industry producing *bidi*, a small roll of dried tobacco. *Bidi* is especially popular in rural communities that may not have access to commercially made cigarettes. It has also become an export product because of the growing demand from Bangladeshis living abroad.

Foreign Minister Morshed Khan of Bangladesh (left) embraces his counterpart from Pakistan, Khurshid Kasuri, before a meeting in Islamabad, July 19, 2004. Relations between their respective countries have not always been so close.

7

Foreign Relations

During the nine-month War of Liberation, the provisional government of Bangladesh outlined a foreign relations plan. Since that time, not surprisingly, circumstances have arisen that compelled changes to the plan, but Bangladesh has generally stuck to its basic principles. Bangladesh's foreign policy is based on nonalignment with major powers, peaceful coexistence with other nations, and opposition to colonialism, *imperialism*, and racism. Bangladesh has maintained a neutral status in international affairs, following the example of countries like Switzerland.

Like any new nation, Bangladesh in the first years after independence considered it essential to establish political roots and achieve recognition throughout the world. That goal has been attained. Today Bangladesh is a member of the United Nations; the Non-Aligned Movement, a 100-member organization of nations committed to resisting the pressures of major powers; the 53-member Commonwealth, an association of independent states that were formerly part of the British Empire; the South Asian Association for Regional Cooperation (SAARC); and the Organization of the Islamic Conference (OIC).

Bangladesh has focused on maintaining strong relations with its South Asian neighbors. It also has strengthened relations with predominantly Muslim countries, the industrialized nations of Western Europe, the United States, Japan, and the People's Republic of China.

Bangladesh and SAARC

Bangladesh was instrumental in forging SAARC, which still struggles to overcome political tensions. In 1980 Ziaur Rahman, then president of Bangladesh, put forward the concept for SAARC: to establish an alliance between Bangladesh, Bhutan, India, the Maldives, Nepal, Pakistan, and Sri Lanka. While they are all located in the same region, these seven countries differ in culture, size, religion, government, and resources. Rahman hoped friendship and understanding among them would accelerate economic development, and that the citizens would benefit. Unfortunately, his vision has not been fully realized.

In 1993 the South Asian Preferential Trading Arrangement was established to promote and sustain mutual trade and economic cooperation among the member countries. Since that time, political tensions among the member nations have slowed the progress of a successful system of intra-regional trade. However, association leaders remain focused on this goal and have formed the SAARC Chamber of Commerce and Industry in an effort to keep intra-regional trade alive in the private business sector. Bangladesh has remained an active participant in SAARC, which still stands as a major foreign relations achievement for the country.

Bangladesh and India

Despite India's early alliance with the struggling Bengali nation in the War of Liberation, relations between India and Bangladesh have often been strained. Disputes over water rights and international borders have arisen many times. The Ganges water issue has been particularly difficult. In 1975 India constructed the Farakka barrage (a dam-like structure that diverts a river's flow) in order to prevent the port of Calcutta from filling up with silt. But the Farakka barrage had severe side effects in southwestern Bangladesh, drying out the land and hurting fishing and agriculture there.

In 1976 the issue was put before the United Nations, which drew up a treaty requiring the two countries to share the dry season flow. Unfortunately, the agreement failed to resolve the conflict until 1996, when the Ganges Water Sharing Treaty was signed.

While the water conflict has died down, India and Bangladesh continue to dispute their borders. In April 2001, for example, 19 Indian and Bangladeshi soldiers were killed in a clash over the border of Meghalaya, a state in the mountainous region of northeast

Soldiers of India's Border Security Force present a gift to Major General Jahangir Alam Chowdhury of Bangladesh before talks in New Delhi on trans-border issues, September 28, 2004. Tensions between Bangladesh and its much larger neighbor have periodically erupted in border clashes.

India. Bangladesh protested the construction of a road along the border, claiming that India has illegally dominated the area since 1971. After three days of negotiations, Bangladesh agreed to leave the territory under Indian authority, as long as India dismantled the road in the disputed area.

Other Regional Neighbors

Relations between Bangladesh and Pakistan were understandably strained in the immediate aftermath of the 1971 war. By 1974, however, the two countries had established diplomatic ties. In the years since, mutual interests such as the strengthening of ties with Western countries, as well as their shared Islamic heritage, have drawn Pakistan and Bangladesh closer together.

Nepal and Bangladesh enjoy a mutually beneficial relationship. Bangladesh needs Nepal's cooperation in increasing the flow of the Ganges, as well as in controlling the terrible floods that devastate Bangladesh. In exchange for this assistance, Bangladesh offers port access to Nepal, reducing its dependence on the Indian port of Calcutta. The other SAARC members also enjoy generally cordial relations with Bangladesh.

Bangladesh and the United States

As a member of the Non-Aligned Movement, Bangladesh has steadfastly avoided military ties with the United States. But it has looked to Washington for food aid and trade relations.

For its part, the United States was reluctant to embrace the newly established People's Republic of Bangladesh, which gained its independence during a time when Cold War tensions were high. Not only did Bangladesh seem to be leaning toward socialism, but the Soviet Union—America's Cold War nemesis—was an active supporter of the new nation.

In 1974 the United States briefly cut off food and other aid when Bangladesh signed a trade agreement with Cuba, a Soviet ally under an American trade embargo, to export jute bags. Once Bangladesh cancelled its deal with Cuba, however, U.S. aid was resumed.

Losing the trade agreement with Cuba did little to damage the Bangladeshi economy. Soon Bangladesh had increased its exports to the United States, which became the biggest buyer of Bangladeshi ready-made garments. At present, the export of these garments keeps the balance of trade with the United States in Bangladesh's favor. Since natural gas deposits have been discovered, the United States has taken an even greater interest in the country.

Members of a Bangladeshi Islamic fundamentalist group called Bangladesh Khelafat Andolon protest the U.S. military offensive in Fallujah, Iraq, November 12, 2004. Some Western experts worry that, with its extreme poverty and its overwhelmingly Muslim population, Bangladesh might prove fertile ground for Islamic extremism.

Other Foreign Relations

Great Britain, Germany, and the Scandinavian countries have relations of varying levels of commitment with Bangladesh. These countries are involved in projects such as technical training, flood control, rural development, and infrastructure development in Bangladesh.

During the War of Liberation, Bangladesh's relations with the Soviet Union were very important. In fact, Sheikh Mujibur Rahman made the Soviet Union the destination of his first overseas visit. That and other friendly overtures suggested to many international observers that Bangladesh was moving toward the Soviet camp. However, this impression did not last following the overthrow of Sheikh Mujib. Today, relations with Russia are improving, and Bangladesh recently took steps to purchase Russian military equipment.

As soon as Bangladesh gained independence, it initiated relations with predominantly Muslim countries. With Pakistan continually discharging anti-Bangladesh propaganda, establishing positive foreign relations with the Arab world was considered critical. The approach soon paid off: when an oil embargo imposed in 1973 produced windfall profits for the petroleum-exporting Arab countries, they channeled aid funds to Bangladesh, along with other developing countries in Asia and Africa. Today many skilled and unskilled Bangladeshis find work in Arab countries. In disputes between Arab states and their rivals, Bangladesh has always been a strong supporter of the Arab side, though it has avoided direct involvement.

Foreign policy between Bangladesh and Japan is based primarily on economic interests. Japan is the second-largest provider of financial assistance to Bangladesh. Bangladesh, for its part, imports many Japanese products, and Japanese investors have supported the Karnaphuli Fertilizer Company and expressed interest in helping set up export ventures in Bangladesh.

China, like the United States, opposed the War of Liberation. However, while the United States did not maintain its stance following Bangladesh's independence, China created several obstacles for the new country. First, it vetoed Bangladesh's admission into the United Nations in 1972. Second, it refused to recognize Bangladesh, siding with Pakistan and referring to the new country as a land under Indian occupation. By 1974 Pakistan and India had established diplomatic relations with Bangladesh, and a year later China followed suit. Today, Bangladesh and China cooperate on military and economic affairs, and China supplies weapons and training to the Bangladeshi armed forces.

Foreign Aid

Throughout its existence as an independent nation, Bangladesh has relied on foreign aid as a means of financing development. When Bangladesh broke away from Pakistan, it also left behind its economic foundation. The country's early years were marked by financial hardship. Industrial production was practically at a standstill, agricultural output had declined significantly, and normal trading activities were sluggish. If the international community had not infused a massive flow of foreign aid into the economic veins of the new country, Bangladesh probably would not have survived.

Bangladesh continues to receive substantial economic aid—an estimated $1.575 billion worth in 2000—from a variety of international sources. Foreign aid has come from Japan, China, Saudi Arabia, and the major Western countries. In addition, agencies and foundations such as the Ford Foundation, UNICEF and other UN agencies, and the Asia Foundation have helped Bangladesh.

Foreign aid involves food aid, grants, long- and short-term loans, and technical assistance. Food aid includes foodstuffs (mostly wheat), as well as their transport, storage, and distribution. Many loans have supplied

Bangladesh has experienced considerable turmoil during its brief time as an independent state, but observers hope that a developing economy and increased political stability will produce a better future for the country's people.

consumer items and industrial raw materials. Some grants have furnished financial and physical aid for projects such as hydroelectric power and oil and gas exploration.

Since the 1990s a large part of Bangladesh's foreign policy has centered on maintaining good relations with donor nations and private donors who assist in moving the economy forward. Balancing the country's imports and exports has also been a long-term goal. Although Bangladesh's imports still outweigh its exports, the trade deficit is narrowing. Malls in America, shops in Europe, and bazaars and outdoor markets in the Middle East all sell articles of clothing labeled "Made in Bangladesh." These clothes, along with such products as leather goods and frozen foods, are helping Bangladesh increase its export earnings—and, perhaps, lay the foundation for a more prosperous and more stable country.

pre-3rd century B.C.	The Vanga kingdom, first alluded to in ancient Hindu writings, rules the Bangladesh region.
324–185 B.C.	The Mauryan Empire controls Bengal and introduces Buddhism to the region.
ca. A.D. **320–550**	The Gupta Empire rules Bengal; Hindu social and religious practices are instituted.
mid-700s	Pala dynasty rulers come to power and begin founding Buddhist monasteries and schools.
1001–1030	Muslim armies of Mahmud of Ghazni raid the Indian subcontinent.
1050	The Sena dynasty gains power and reinstates the Hindu religion.
1199	Mohammed Bakhtiar captures Bengal and incorporates the area into the Delhi Sultanate; Islam gains a foothold.
1206	Most of northern India and Bengal becomes part of Delhi Sultanate.
1341–1576	After Bengal gains independence from the Delhi Sultanate, individual Muslim rulers govern parts of Bengal and its neighboring states.
1576	Akbar and his Muslim armies conquer Bengal, establishing the Mughal Empire.
1600s	The majority of the East Bengal population converts to Islam; European traders set up outposts, control trade with India and the Far East, and set up jute-processing operations in Bengal.
1686	The British East India Company founds Calcutta.
early 1700s	The Mughal Empire declines; local nawabs increase their control.

Chronology

mid-18th century	Great Britain begins building an empire on the Indian subcontinent, designating Bengal as a major commercial region.
1757	In the Battle of Plassey, the nawab of Bengal is defeated by British East India forces; Robert Clive and the British East India Company begin to rule Bengal.
1857	The Sepoy Rebellion breaks out; the revolt convinces Great Britain, the following year, to abolish the British East India Company and assume direct control on the Indian subcontinent.
1905	East and West Bengal are partitioned.
1906	The Muslim League is formed.
1911	East and West Bengal are reunited.
1930–40	The Muslim League raises demands for a separate Muslim state.
1947	In the partition of India following the end of British rule, East Bengal becomes East Pakistan, part of the new Muslim-majority country of Pakistan; fighting breaks out between India and Pakistan over contested regions.
1952	On February 21, police fire on marchers, killing several students protesting the government decision to ban Bangla, the Bengali language.
1954	The Awami League is formed to fight for Bengali causes.
1966	Sheikh Mujibur Rahman presents his six-point program for East Pakistani self-rule.

1970	A devastating cyclone kills 266,000 Bengalis; the Awami League wins a majority of the National Assembly seats; the West Pakistani government refuses East Pakistan's claims to self-government.
1971	On March 25, the president of Pakistan sends troops to stop Bengali protests; Sheikh Mujibur Rahman is arrested and the Awami League is banned; East Pakistan declares its independence, marking the beginning of the nine-month War of Liberation; on December 16, Pakistan surrenders to the Indian army.
1972	Rahman becomes prime minister of the People's Republic of Bangladesh; a constitution is adopted.
1974	Rahman declares a state of emergency in December.
1975	Rahman becomes president and makes his political party the only legitimate one in government; he is assassinated in August and is replaced by Khondakar Mushtaque Ahmed.
1975	A. S. M. Sayem becomes president and chief martial law administrator (CMLA); the constitution remains suspended.
1976	In November, General Ziaur Rahman (Zia) becomes CMLA.
1977	In April, Zia becomes president as well as CMLA.
1981	On May 30, Zia is assassinated; Justice Abdus Sattar becomes acting president.
1982	Lieutenant General H. M. Ershad removes Sattar in a bloodless coup and names himself CMLA.

Chronology

1983	Ershad names himself president.
1986	Ershad restores political rights; establishes his own political party and runs unopposed for president.
1987	Ershad declares a state of emergency and dissolves Parliament.
1988	Ershad holds new parliamentary elections; Parliament passes a constitutional amendment naming Islam the state religion.
1990	General strikes occur across the country; as law and order deteriorates, Ershad resigns.
1991	Begum Khaleda Zia is elected prime minister in elections considered free and fair; in October, Parliament elects Abdur Rahman Biswas to the presidency.
1994	Strikes and shutdowns take place in opposition to Khaleda Zia's government.
1995	President Abdur Rahman Biswas dissolves Parliament.
1996	In February, Biswas forms a caretaker government and calls for new elections; in June, national elections are held; the Awami League controls Parliament and Sheikh Hasina Wazed becomes prime minister.
2001	The Awami League completes its first five-year tenure as majority in Parliament; in October, Khaleda Zia returns to power as prime minister, heading a coalition government.
2002	Iajuddin Ahmed is sworn in as president.
2004	Widespread flooding between July and September takes more than 700 lives and leaves an estimated 10 million people homeless.

agrarian—relating to farm or rural life.

alluvium—sediment washed down or deposited by rivers as they flow to their mouths.

caretaker government—an interim government that retains power only until elections can be held to establish a permanent government.

caste—a hereditary social class in Hinduism.

coalition—a temporary alliance of distinct political groups or political parties.

commodity—an economic good that is bought and sold (such as an agricultural product).

coup—the sudden overthrow of a government by a small group using violence or the threat of violence.

cyclone—a large-scale storm system with heavy rain and winds similar to a tornado.

delta—a triangle-shaped piece of land formed when sand and soil are deposited at the mouth of a large river.

gross domestic product (GDP)—the total value of all goods and services produced in a country over a one-year period.

imperialism—the practice of extending national power through the political, military, or economic domination of other countries or peoples.

insurgent—a person who rebels agains government authority, especially one who is involved in unconventional warfare such as a guerrilla campaign.

legume—the edible fruit or seed of certain plants, such as peas and beans.

mangrove—a type of tree that grows in wetlands in tropical and subtropical areas and that has support roots extending from its branches.

martial law—law administered by military authorities during periods of national emergency.

Glossary

muslin—a type of cotton fabric.

nawab—a provincial governor of the Mughal Empire (also spelled *nabob*).

patriarchal—relating to a society or culture in which authority, privilege, and power belong predominantly to men.

pulses—any of various plants (such as peas, beans, and lentils) that produce edible seeds.

sediment—material that is transported and deposited by water, wind, or ice.

silt—fine-grained sediment, especially mud or clay particles at the bottom of a river or lake.

steppe—a wide expanse of treeless, usually level, and dry grassland.

Cumming, David. *Bangladesh*. Austin, Tex.: Raintree Steck-Vaughn, 1999.

DK Publishing. *A Life Like Mine*. New York: DK Publishing, 2002.

London, Ellen. *Bangladesh*. Milwaukee, Wisc.: Gareth Stevens Publishers, 2004.

March, Michael. *Bangladesh*. North Mankato, Minn.: Smart Apple Media, 2004.

Montgomery, Sy. *The Man-Eating Tigers of Sundarbans*. Boston: Houghton Mifflin, 2001.

Osborne, Mary Pope. *One World, Many Religions*. New York: Knopf, 1996.

Shrestha, Nanda R. *Nepal and Bangladesh: A Global Studies Handbook*. Santa Barbara, Calif.: ABC-CLIO, 2002.

Whyte, Mariam. *Bangladesh*. New York: Marshall Cavendish, 1999.

Yunus, Muhammad. *Banker to the Poor*. New York: Oxford University Press, 1999.

Internet Resources

http://www.bangladesh-web.com/aboutus.php

An English-language daily news service covering Bangladesh.

http://www.cia.gov/cia/publications/factbook/geos/bg.html

The CIA World Factbook provides a wealth of statistical and background information about Bangladesh.

http://www.virtualbangladesh.com

This easy-to-use site offers the latest news about Bangladesh, pictures, and interactive ways to learn more about the country.

http://www.bangladesh.gov.bd

The official government site for the People's Republic of Bangladesh.

http://www.lonelyplanet.com/destinations/indian_subcontinent/bangladesh/

In addition to being a useful travel guide, this page from Lonely Planet includes informative sections on the culture and history of Bangladesh.

Numbers in **bold italic** refer to captions.

Index

Index

Picture Credits

The **FOREIGN POLICY RESEARCH INSTITUTE (FPRI)** served as editorial consultants for the GROWTH AND INFLUENCE OF ISLAM IN THE NATIONS OF ASIA AND CENTRAL ASIA series. FPRI is one of the nation's oldest "think tanks." The Institute's Middle East Program focuses on Gulf security, monitors the Arab-Israeli peace process, and sponsors an annual conference for teachers on the Middle East, plus periodic briefings on key developments in the region.

Among the FPRI's trustees is a former Secretary of State and a former Secretary of the Navy (and among the FPRI's former trustees and interns, two current Undersecretaries of Defense), not to mention two university presidents emeritus, a foundation president, and several active or retired corporate CEOs.

The scholars of FPRI include a former aide to three U.S. Secretaries of State, a Pulitzer Prize–winning historian, a former president of Swarthmore College and a Bancroft Prize–winning historian, and two former staff members of the National Security Council. And the FPRI counts among its extended network of scholars—especially its Inter-University Study Groups—representatives of diverse disciplines, including political science, history, economics, law, management, religion, sociology, and psychology.

DR. HARVEY SICHERMAN is president and director of the Foreign Policy Research Institute in Philadelphia, Pennsylvania. He has extensive experience in writing, research, and analysis of U.S. foreign and national security policy, both in government and out. He served as Special Assistant to Secretary of State Alexander M. Haig Jr. and as a member of the Policy Planning Staff of Secretary of State James A. Baker III. Dr. Sicherman was also a consultant to Secretary of the Navy John F. Lehman Jr. (1982–1987) and Secretary of State George Shultz (1988).

A graduate of the University of Scranton (B.S., History, 1966), Dr. Sicherman earned his Ph.D. at the University of Pennsylvania (Political Science, 1971), where he received a Salvatori Fellowship. He is author or editor of numerous books and articles, including *America the Vulnerable: Our Military Problems and How to Fix Them* (FPRI, 2002) and *Palestinian Autonomy, Self-Government and Peace* (Westview Press, 1993). He edits *Peacefacts*, an FPRI bulletin that monitors the Arab-Israeli peace process.

DORIS VALLIANT is an English teacher who lives in Easton, Maryland. She writes books for young people and magazine articles for regional publications.